WOMEN IN THE MARTIAL ARTS

A NEW SPIRIT RISING

WOMEN IN THE MARTIAL ARTS

A NEW SPIRIT RISING

Illustrated with photographs
LINDA ATKINSON

DODD, MEAD & COMPANY—New York

B.C.E., "Before the Common Era," is an alternative dating system that maintains the same numbering as the older B.C. but is intended to be more universal in its denotation.

PHOTOCREDITS
Courtesy of Beth Austin, pp. 142 (photo by James Ruebsamen), 146, 149, 153, 156, 158; courtesy of Banshee, p. 20; photos by R. J. Bassano, pp. 28, 37, 39, 42, 44; photo by Eva Blinder, p. 91; courtesy of Pattie Dacanay, pp. 84, 86, 88, 94, 96; photo by Valerie Eads, p. 11; courtesy of Valerie Eads, p. 7; courtesy of Annie Ellman, p. 48; courtesy of Gerry Fifer, pp. 9, 13, 14, 18, 19; photo by Donna Deborah Gray, p. 63; photos by Morgan Gwenwald, pp. 16, 50, 53; courtesy of Kanagawa Prefectural Museum, Yokahama, and Valerie Eads, p. 5; courtesy of Rusty Kanokogi, p. 34; photos by Carol Lewis, pp. 56, 61, 165, 168, 170, 171, 173; photos by M. E. McCourt, pp. 122, 127, 135, 138; photo by Peter Perazio, p. 26; photos by Nancy Rosenblum, pp. 68, 72, 77, 79; photo by Jean Shaffer, p. 59; photos by Laurie Usher, pp. 102, 105, 109, 111, 115, 116; Craig Wahlstrom, p. 162.

1 2 3 4 5 6 7 8 9 10

Library of Congress Cataloging in Publication Data

Atkinson, Linda.
    Women in the martial arts.

    Bibliography: p.
    Includes index.
    1. Hand-to-hand fighting, Oriental.   2. Sports for
women.   I. Title.
GV1112.A86   1983   796.8'15'088042   83-16302
ISBN 0-396-08223-8
ISBN 0-396-08297-1 (pbk.)

For my sisters
MIRIAM and EDNA,
with love

Contents

Note to the Reader   ix

Women in the Martial Arts   1

Judo   23
RUSTY KANOKOGI

Karate   46
ANNIE ELLMAN

Kung Fu   65
LAVERNE BATES

T'ai Chi Chuan   82
PATTIE DACANAY

Tae Kwon Do   100
SUNNY GRAFF

Kendo   119
VALERIE EADS

Aikido   140
BETH AUSTIN

The Universal Way   160
TONIE HARRIS

Suggestions for Further Reading   176

Resources   177

Index   178

Acknowledgments   181

Note to
the Reader

I FIRST FOUND MY WAY TO A KARATE SCHOOL BECAUSE OF A FLYER SOME-one had posted on a fence near the supermarket where I shop. I was thirty-nine years old, the mother of two children, and absolutely amazed.

I arrived early for the first class. People were warming up on their own. One woman was striking a punching bag that hung from the ceiling on a heavy chain. From time to time, she let out loud, startling shrieks. I looked at her for signs of self-consciousness, some recognition on her part that everyone could hear her, but she seemed to be in another world. Closer to me, a young woman was breathing deeply, sending slow-motion, tension-filled punches into the air. Her arm trembled as she worked, as if she were pushing against an object of great weight. Another woman practiced a kick of rib-cage height over and over again, closely watching herself in a mirror.

As I looked around the room, I realized that all the women had a sense about themselves that I had never seen before. There was something serious and unselfconscious in the way they moved and worked, and it was a relief to be among them. As I watched, I couldn't help wondering how they had all come to be here. I think I started to want to write this book at that moment.

That day I began to train in karate, and I still take classes regularly. Karate has become important to my life in ways that I did not anticipate when I began. I can no longer imagine myself without it. And the more involved I become, the harder it is to remember that most women still think of karate and the martial arts, when they think about them at all, as activities for "other people."

I never learned who put the flyer up, but I will always be thankful that she did. It helped me to find something wonderful. I hope this book will be like that flyer.

—Linda Atkinson

Women in the Martial Arts

THE MARTIAL ARTS ARE FIGHTING ARTS: HAND-TO-HAND, MOSTLY WEAPON-less, designed to be used in self-defense against one or more individual attackers. They rely on technique rather than muscle power, so they minimize the natural advantage of people who are bigger and stronger than others. Most of the arts don't require equipment or anything else that money can buy. They use the body itself. They train it, refine it, develop its capacities from the inside out. The martial arts may be the most effective fighting systems ever designed. But their meaning and value are not confined to fighting. They tap and develop energy most people are not aware of having. They change our ideas of what is possible and show us that we are capable of being stronger, more courageous, better than we ever dreamed.

The martial arts are based on ancient Asian fighting systems, some of which can be traced back to the Chou Dynasty, which ruled China from 1122 to 255 B.C.E. Although hand-to-hand fighting systems have been found in many parts of the world, only in Asia did they develop into arts: complex, formal disciplines in which spiritual and physical dimensions merged. And although the phrase "martial arts" is not a technical one, and can be used to refer to any and all kinds of fighting, it is most common and quite proper

1

to reserve it, as it is reserved here, for the unique and fascinating fighting arts of Asia.

Most of the details about the development of the martial arts have been lost to history, but scholars agree that the arts began during the seventh century in the Buddhist monasteries of China. Both women and men lived in these communities, and both took part in the development of the arts. Perhaps, as author Maxine Hong Kingston wondered in *The Woman Warrior*, women's feet were later bound because they were once so dangerous.

Shaolin Temple, in the northern forests of Hunan Province, was at the center of the development. According to some sources, Bodhidharma himself, the founder of Zen Buddhism, came to Shaolin from India in 525, bringing with him the principles that inspired the martial arts. No one can be sure of this, but it is known that during the seventh century, Shaolin Temple fighting became famous and that before the century was over, it was being practiced by people in Buddhist communities all over China. It had become something quite distinctive—a fighting art with characteristics all its own.

Practical fighting skills were at the heart of Shaolin fighting, but the emphasis was not entirely practical. Fighting techniques, combined with Indian breathing techniques and the principles of Chinese medicine, were infused with Buddhist visions of reality and Taoist beliefs about the harmony and balance of nature that can be traced back to Lao Tsu, a sage of the sixth century B.C.E. Physical development was connected to spiritual development. Fighting forms—stances, blocks, strikes, ways of moving toward and away from an opponent—were practiced for their own sakes. Physical exercise became "meditation in motion."

Powerful fighters emerged, people with extraordinary abilities to sense what other people could not sense and to react to threats and danger in ways that made them seem invincible. But the goal of the training was not simply victory in a fight. It was to find and tap the energy of life itself, to explore the nature and limits of human power, to deepen and strengthen our connections to life and to the forces that move the universe.

In the centuries that followed, the Chinese fighting arts—for there were soon many styles and methods in addition to the one that originated at Shaolin—spread throughout the Asian world. Wherever they took hold—Okinawa, Korea, Japan, Indonesia, Malaysia, the Philippines, Burma, India, Pakistan, Thailand—they were modified to meet the needs of the people who learned them. New styles were created, and new arts. As yet very little is known about the extent to which women participated in the arts in most of these lands. Historians are just beginning to investigate the roles played by women in history. But folk tales and myths are filled with stories of strong women who led their people into battle against despots and tyrants and who fought courageously in the field. These stories suggest a tradition of women warriors and make it seem likely that women participated in the martial arts as they developed.

In Chinese history, about which more is known—China having been the subject of intense interest to Western traders, missionaries, and governments for several centuries—there are many accounts of women who led peasant rebellions and who were fearsome warriors and even rulers. Perhaps the most widely loved of China's women warriors was the fabulous Fa Mulan ("Magnolia"), a young woman of the sixth century who took her father's place in battle and whose heroism is celebrated in folk songs and tales that are popular to this very day. Chinese oral tradition acknowledges women among the masters of kung fu, and women are credited with the creation of several important kung fu styles. White crane boxing, developed in the eighteenth century, is one. *Wing-chun* kung fu, developed in the sixteenth century is another. *Wing-chun*, created by a Buddhist nun and named for her most brilliant student (*wing-chun* means "beautiful springtime") became especially popular in the United States because it was the style with which Bruce Lee began his career as a martial artist.

In Japan, women born into the warrior, or samurai, class, which flourished from the tenth to the eighteenth centuries, often learned to fight alongside their brothers. They were expected to learn to use a variety of samurai weapons, especially the curved sword called the *naginata*, which hung above the doorway in most samurai households. With propellor-like slashes, the *naginata* could be wielded against an enemy on horseback or on foot.

Although fighters in the field were normally men, it was not unheard of for a woman to join them in battle or sometimes to lead them. Itagaki, a woman of the thirteenth century, led three thousand warriors of the Taira clan against ten thousand soldiers the Hojo clan sent to crush them. Her courage was honored by her warriors and her skill was recorded even by her enemies. Tomoé, a woman of the same period, was said to be a match for one hundred warriors.

By the 1700s, however, except for the art of *naginata*, which had become a woman's art exclusively, the martial arts were almost entirely off-limits even to Japanese women. Peace had finally come to Japan, so the warrior class was losing its reason for being, and the tradition of women as fighters was losing ground too. In an effort to retain what was most valuable about the martial arts, the deadlier techniques were discarded and new forms emerged that stressed the spiritual values behind them. But as the martial arts moved indoors, from real battles for life and death to sparring matches in safely supervised schools, the schools closed their doors to women. The art of judo, based on the strictly-for-combat jujutsu, was created by Jigaro Kano, a thoughtful man who wished to promote the moral, social, and spiritual values that he thought were inherent in martial art training. Nevertheless, when he opened his school, the Kodokan, in 1882, it was for men only.

Until the Second World War, the martial arts were almost un-

The Fighting Women's Army of Kagoshima, *a woodblock print by Nagayama Umosu commemorating an actual battle that took place during the last samurai rebellion in April, 1877.*

known outside of Asia. But in the 1940s and early 1950s, thousands of soldiers stationed in Korea and Japan saw and studied judo, karate, tae kwon do, and some of the lesser-known arts with traditional masters. When they returned home, they brought their skills, their excitement, and sometimes their teachers with them. No country greeted them with more enthusiasm than the United States.

Robert Trias, a navy man who learned karate during a tour of duty in Japan, opened the first American Karate school in Phoenix, Arizona, in 1946. In 1948, he founded the United States Karate Association. In 1951, the Strategic Air Command sent physical education trainers to Japan to study the arts and design programs for members of the American armed forces. In 1953, a team of high-ranking Japanese martial artists was invited to Washington for a series of demonstrations and seminars. The same year, the first public martial arts exposition ever held in the United States took place when Mas Oyama, a Korean tae kwon do master,

brought the audience in Madison Square Garden to its feet with
stunning displays of astonishing techniques. Oyama became
something of a legend for fighting bulls (scheduled for slaughter)
with his bare hands. He could stop a charging bull with an out-
stretched arm and kill it with a single blow.

By the mid-1950s, the martial arts had captured the imaginations
of thousands of Americans. Before the decade was over, there
wasn't a big city or a small one that didn't have at least one training
hall for one martial art or another. By 1964, judo had been admitted
to the Olympics, Bruce Lee was the kung fu hero of a new TV series
called the "Green Hornet," and the martial arts were being touted
and praised by people everywhere. They were great for self-
defense! They were great for keeping fit! They were great for peace
of mind! They were great for everyone—young, old, big, small,
athletic, non-athletic—everyone could train in a martial art!
Everyone, that is, except women.

A woman martial artist? A woman who was a strong, self-
confident fighter? In the fifties and early sixties, it was almost
unthinkable. Women athletes were still greeted with surprise, in
spite of people like Gertrude Ederle, who had not only swum the
English Channel in 1926, but had swum it two hours faster than any
male swimmer had ever done, Babe Didrikson Zaharias, who
excelled in every sport she ever tried and won two gold medals in
the track and field events at the 1932 Olympics, and others. Fine
women athletes were considered exceptional, not representative.
The ideal woman, in the first half of the twentieth century, was
neither strong nor athletic, and girls who liked sports and physically challenging activities were still said to be acting like boys.

The issue of women and sports was often couched in physical
terms—as though women's bodies were not and could not be up to
snuff. But, as Dorothy Harris, Director of the Center for Women
and Sport at Pennsylvania State University, noted in 1976, the
"number one problem" facing women has never been physical. It

Kobayashi Seiko (1900–1981) practicing kendo-no-kata *with her uncle. She was the tenth generation leader of* Bukko Ryo, *a style of kendo. Her father, kendo teacher Chiba Chosaku, is watching.*

is social. It is "the behavior expected of females by society." As Margaret Dunckle wrote in a 1975 booklet prepared for the federal government's Project on the Status and Education of Women, women and girls have not been encouraged to be athletes because "the traits associated with athletic excellence—achievement, self-confidence, aggressiveness, leadership, strength, swiftness—are often seen as being in contradiction with the role of women."

"But I can beat him," said the confused daughter on a 1960s TV series called "My World and Welcome to It." "You mean I'm supposed to let him win?"

"I think," said her mother, "that it would be the feminine thing to do."

Male officials in the world of sports have been among the most ardent champions of the view that women cannot and should not participate in the full range of athletic events. In 1967, Kathrine

Switzer became the first woman to run an official public marathon when she snuck into the "for men only" Boston Marathon. She was chased down the track by an outraged official after he realized that a fragile you-know-what was out there running with the men. Kathrine completed the twenty-six miles easily and was thereupon suspended from the Amateur Athletic Union because women—for their own good, of course—were not allowed to run races longer than one and a half miles. "Men," wrote Janice Kaplan in her book *Women and Sports,* "sometimes seem more ready to accept women as brain surgeons than as athletes."

But if women athletes contradicted some of society's basic assumptions about "female nature," women fighters were beyond the pale entirely. Nevertheless, some extraordinary women managed to find their way into the martial arts even in the 1950s. Rusty Kanokogi, who was to become the leading woman judo player in America, began to train in 1955. She used a broom closet to change clothes in because there weren't any dressing rooms for women. (Except for Rusty, there weren't any women.) But in the late sixties and early seventies, when so many forces for change were at work in the United States and around the world, women began turning to the martial arts in greater and greater numbers. In the beginning, most of them were directly inspired by the women's liberation movement. They entered the arts to learn self-defense, to step out of the "passive-victim" role, to find out what their limits really were, and to begin the process of changing a society in which women were so often the targets and victims of violence.

"It is legitimate to ask whether teaching women to punch and kick could bring change on any meaningful level," wrote Nadia Telsey, one of the first women to study karate in the United States and a thoughtful analyst of the meaning of martial arts training for women. "Surely we cannot expect to end violence against women by taking on our attackers one by one. Yet each woman learns about violence as an individual and it is as individuals that we must begin to fight back."

They found in the martial arts even more than they had hoped to find.

"Karate is above all empowering," Nadia wrote. "It acquaints us with our bodies, giving us evidence of our own strength, which is often surprising to us. It enables us to act from our own bodies, speak with our own words. 'Femininity' can no longer limit us. On the most obvious level, karate provides us with the physical skills we need to fend off assault. Far beyond this, it gives us a sense of control over our own destinies."

Even the women who were not directly involved in the women's movement were encouraged by the atmosphere it created, an atmosphere in which it was all right for women to become fit and

For many women, learning to fight has been both difficult and exhilarating.

strong and to use their bodies, not just decorate them. All the women who stayed in the martial arts, those who called themselves feminists and those who did not, stayed because they came to love the arts on many levels, though the obstacles they faced were difficult and seemed at times to be endless. For most people in the sixties and seventies, even a woman marathon runner was not entirely legitimate. A woman martial artist was definitely going too far.

"In many schools, just getting the men to acknowledge the existence of women students was like pulling teeth," says Susan Ribner, also one of the first women to enter the all-male karate world in New York in the 1960s. "Even with women present, the instructors would end classes with oaths like, 'We are proud to be karate men.' "

In one school, a sign just inside the door said: "No smoking, no alcohol, no women." A woman who complained was told that if she didn't like it, she could leave.

In some schools, women were kept out of certain parts of the training and "excused" from certain exercises on the grounds that they wouldn't be able to do them or would be injured in strange and sometimes mythical ways.

"Women off the floor!" was the standard command at one school when the time came for push-ups. To the woman who asked for permission to stay, the instructor explained that push-ups would be "bad for her reproductive organs."

In another school, women were allowed to do push-ups, but only half the number required of men. In still another, they were allowed to do the same number of push-ups, but only half the sit-ups!

One teacher refused to let his black belt men spar with women because he thought it would ruin the men's style. In another, the instructor wouldn't let women spar at all because they had too many "soft spots" on their bodies.

Achieving the commitment and focus shown in this strike and kiai *to the bag takes a long time.*

"Sometimes I wanted to go back to the role that was familiar to me, even though I knew I was better and more capable than that role allowed," said one woman about her early training. "Being a 'first' is very exciting but it's also frightening. We weren't sure of what the end of our story would be."

They were, as Kathrine Switzer said of the first women to run in marathons, "sailing on a flat earth."

"We were in a real quandry," Sue Ribner recalls. "We didn't know how far women could go or what we could really hope to achieve, and most teachers were not interested in helping us to find out. They didn't mind training women—it brought in money—but that wasn't where they expected to find excellence. We had to set our own standards, because there were no standards for us except humiliating ones."

In most schools that had women students, the women came to see themselves as belonging to an underground.

"When the instructor says women should stop doing an exercise before the men stop, pretend you don't hear," was the advice given newer women. "If your instructor tells you to stop because he thinks you've done enough, say 'No, I'm all right,' and go on working."

"Until it becomes clear exactly what women's potential is," Sue wrote in an article for *The Sportswoman*, "our sights must be set at the highest level. Otherwise, our true ability may never be discovered."

In 1972, when the trickle of women into the martial arts schools had become a steady stream, women in New York—Sue Ribner and Nadia Telsey among them—formed the Women's Martial Arts Union. It was the first organization of its kind in the United States and probably in the world. Its top priority was to help women martial artists of whatever art or style meet one another, share their skills and problems, and end the isolation each of them felt in their separate schools. The women who came together to form the union had themselves met by accident, after a judo player noticed the *gi* another woman was carrying as they waited on the same subway platform for a train.

"It was a karate *gi*," Gerry Fifer, the judo player, recalls, "tied in a green belt. I had been training in judo for almost a year, and I was dying to meet other women who were in the martial arts. Finally, when the train didn't come, I got my courage up and introduced myself—as fast as I could, so she wouldn't think I was a lunatic— telling this perfect stranger in about two seconds that I knew that what she was carrying was a karate *gi* because I myself was studying judo, that I didn't know any other women training in anything, and where was she training and what was it like there?"

The woman invited Gerry to come with her to her karate school, where Susan Ribner and a handful of other women were also

Core of the Women's Martial Arts Union. From left: *Kathleen Ahern; Mary Lutz; Eva Blinder; Nadia Telsey; Susan Ribner; Gerry Fifer.*

training. Shortly after that, Gerry met a woman in night school who was training in aikido, and slowly a network formed. Realizing how important and how difficult it was for women martial artists to meet one another, they decided to set up a union. They would meet regularly, share self-defense skills, hold workshops, talk about the problems they were having in their schools or with their training.

"We really needed to make connections with one another and support one another," Gerry recalls. "Especially in the beginning, it was because we had one another that we could stick it out."

One of the issues for many of the women was violence itself. Were they endorsing violence by learning a martial art? Were they themselves becoming part of the "culture of violence?"

"Not knowing how to stop violence doesn't diminish violence," Nadia wrote later. "We use karate to help each other develop

Eva Blinder and Kathleen Ahern of the Women's Martial Arts Union demonstrate karate skills in Central Park.

confidence, conquer fear, be stronger and more self-reliant persons."

"Historically," Sue noted, "women have been kept in their place by an excessive fear of physical violence. Women take up the martial arts to demystify violence and conquer their fear of it, not because they themselves want to become violent people who attack nice men on their way to work."

"It isn't an accident," says Annie Ellman, a founder and chief instructor of one of the oldest karate schools for women in the United States, "that women, children and older people are the most frequently attacked people in our society. Assailants expect us to be weak and defenseless—good targets. Every time we fight back and resist attacks and violence, we help destroy the myth of women as passive and helpless and make the world safer for all women."

There aren't many statistics about the effectiveness of self-defense training, since statistics are collected about crimes that occur, not about crimes that do not occur. But feedback from students of the martial arts and of self-defense courses based on martial arts techniques is just about unanimous in its praise for the skills and strengths imparted. Every self-defense teacher has heard countless stories of students and former students who successfully resisted attack as a result of their training. Many studies support these claims. One, conducted by Dr. Frank Javorek of the Denver General Hospital Crime Prevention Unit, noted that women escaped weaponless attackers over 85 percent of the time if they yelled to attract attention *and* resisted the attack. Women who did only one of these things escaped 50 percent of the time. Women who did neither rarely escaped. In another study, Dr. James Selkin found that in weaponless assaults, the sooner a woman resisted, the greater her chances of escaping. In still another study, assailants admitted that their victims' fears—as shown in crying, nervousness, verbal stalling and pleading—encouraged them to go on with their assault. Another explained that assailants often engaged in an informal "selection" process. They tend to choose as victims women who look vulnerable and to bypass those who, because of their physical appearance, assertive body language and wary, suspicious attitudes seem as though they would not make easy victims. Self-defense training, by giving women skills, not only gives them real options and things to do if assaulted, but gives them confidence—which in itself takes them out of the ranks of women who look like good targets.

Within months of its founding, members of the Women's Martial Arts Union were demonstrating in schools, at public events, and

At a street fair in Brooklyn, children from Brooklyn Women's Martial Arts give a demonstration.

top: The moment before beginning a kata, *an imaginary fight, the eyes are closed to help summon one's concentration and fighting spirit. Annie Ellman, the instructor, tells her students to visualize the* kata *they are about to perform and to be ready for anything when they open their eyes.*

middle: Part of the kata

political rallies. They tried to make themselves as visible as possible in order to change the image of the martial arts as exclusively male and to encourage other women to join. They gave interviews, held workshops, wrote articles for the press. They explained the arts and what each had to offer women, suggesting ways to deal with the problems they might find in martial arts schools.

"Make sure women are taken seriously in whatever class you attend," cautioned the Union's *Guide to Self-Defense,* published in 1973. "The demands on men and women should be equal. Stay away from classes which exclude women from the sparring. The instructor should make no disparaging remarks about women and neither should women be singled out or praised for every small thing."

The guide advised women to "try to be stoic, even if the class is difficult. Don't allow yourself to be coddled. Usually women's endurance is equal to, if not better than men's. If you have a little trouble in the beginning, hold on, try harder, and you'll get it."

As far as competitive events were concerned, some arts made room for women with relative ease—not without effort on the part of the first women practitioners, but without a great deal of hullabaloo. Kendo, for example, integrated women into matches and allowed them full access to competitive events, dividing partici-

bottom: A kiai *is part of the kata*

No place was off limits. Judo players from the Women's Martial Arts Union demonstrate before a lunch-hour crowd in the financial district in New York City, early 1970s.

pants into categories based on weight but not gender. Others were committed to keeping women out of competitive events, or to keeping them from competing against men. The first women to enter judo, for example, remained on the sidelines until they organized their own events and competitions. The separation of the sexes remains the rule in competitive judo, tae kwon do, and some of the other arts today. In karate, there have been as many different policies regarding women as there are schools and associations. At some times, in some places, women have been allowed to fight against men. At other times, they have not been allowed to fight competitively at all—not even against other women. The rationale behind the policies hasn't always been clear and there is no way to be certain of what the rules will be in the future.

In December, 1972, at Richmond College on Staten Island, the Women's Martial Arts Union held a weekend training and planning session for women in the martial arts, the first of its kind anywhere. Workshops were given in the various arts, and seminars were held to discuss problems and ideas about training. Over one hundred women from as far away as Washington, D.C., attended the session. A second training session was held in Greeley,

Pennsylvania, in 1973, and a third was held in 1974 in Oswego, New York.

The Women's Martial Arts Union disbanded a few years later, but it left behind a network of women martial artists which crisscrossed the country. Training weekends and teachers' conferences have been held almost every year since 1974, sponsored and organized by a different school and a different teacher each time.

In 1981, a new organization was formed, the National Women's Martial Arts Federation. Its membership included many of the same women who had been in the union. In June, 1982, under the direction of Banshee, fourth-degree black belt in *Uechi-Ryu* karate,

A judo throw at the first special training session for women, on Staten Island.

Participants at the Special Training Weekend in Provincetown, 1982.

the federation organized a Special Training Weekend in Province-town, Massachusetts. It drew almost four hundred women from all over the country, representing twenty-six different fighting systems.

On the last night of the four-day weekend, a demonstration was held in the town hall. Schools and individual artists presented their forms and skills. Unlike the other parts of the Special Training Weekend, this event was open to members of the public—the townspeople who had been so cordial to and so intrigued by the hundreds of women in *gi's* and assorted martial outfits whom they had seen working out on beaches, jogging along roadways, filling restaurants, and poring through gift shops on Commercial Street.

Some of the presentations on the stage that night were as exciting and dramatic as anything that has ever been presented on any stage. There were sword dances based on ancient Chinese sword techniques, inspired by poetry and put to music by Master Bow-Sim Mark, Director of the Chinese Wushu Research Institute of Boston. There was stick fighting, sword fighting, board breaking, full-contact sparring, a weapons display by Roberta Trias Kelly—daughter of Robert Trias—in which sparks flashed and metal clashed ominously, and a Bruce Lee scenario in which Barbara Niggle, a Grand Champion of the United States Karate Association, took on four opponents and sent them flying with a rush of leaps and a volley of kicks and punches executed faster than most people in the audience could follow.

But for many of the women there that night, the most memorable moment came toward the end of the presentations. Instructor Roberta Schine and students from her New York Karate School for Women were on the stage. Roberta was reading statements made by women at earlier special training sessions. Her students were following the statements with short dramatizations.

Suddenly, the lights were turned off and the stage was black. Then a spotlight focused on Roberta. She looked at her paper and then out at the audience.

"It says here—" she smiled and held up the paper "—that Sue Ribner decided to take karate when someone told her it was too hard for women!"

The audience laughed.

"She was expelled from her first school because she insisted that women be allowed to do knuckle push-ups!"

The audience cheered.

Roberta stepped back, her hands at her sides, and waited until the audience was quiet. Then she took a quick step forward, grabbed the microphone and boomed, "Her instructor said, *Susan! Don't you know! Women don't do knuckle push-ups!*"

Drums rolled and the audience yelled as the spotlight flashed on two of Roberta's students who leaped to center stage and took push-up positions. The drums began to pound and the audience, on its feet, counted with them— "One! Two! Three! Four!"—nearly drowning them out as they cheered for the women on stage, for Roberta, for Sue, and, it seemed, for every woman who was ever told she couldn't do things, for every woman who was ever stopped from trying.

The martial arts operate on many different levels. They are ways of becoming fit and strong, ways of developing fighting skills, ways of learning discipline and focus, ways of meditating, ways of playing. Different arts stress different things, but all of them derive from the understanding that physical and spiritual strengths go together and are within our power to effect—to increase, develop, improve without end. All of them ask practitioners to test the limits they think define them, challenge those limits and go beyond them. For the men who have known and loved them, the martial arts have always been inspiring. For western women, the martial arts are an invitation to new and truer visions of themselves and of what they may hope to be.

The women in this book are among the first outside of Asia to reach advanced levels in the martial arts. Some came to the arts for personal reasons, some for political reasons, and some happened in by accident. All of them have broken through the stereotypes to show us a little of what is on the other side: the courage and strength of women, the joy and power of the human spirit when it is free. Here are their stories.

Judo

JUDO IS THE MARTIAL ART IN WHICH YOU LEARN TO THROW AN OPPONENT to the ground, hold her down, and keep her immobilized. You also learn how to avoid getting thrown yourself, and how to escape from the holds and locks someone may try to use on you.

Ju means "yielding," and *do* means "the way." Judo, the way of yielding, is based on the idea that it is better to move with a physical force that is directed against you than to block it with a force of your own. You yield to your opponent's force and "break" his balance while you keep him moving—through the air and down onto the mat if you can. Judo techniques are based on the principles of leverage and the law of gravity. They are precise and exact, and when performed correctly, they always work.

Judo is a strong and ingenious system, and basic judo techniques are included in most self-defense courses. When properly practiced in a training hall, in spite of all the flips and falls, partners are hardly ever injured. Judo skills include falling without getting hurt. It is part of basic judo ethics to protect your partner even when you throw her down. What you do isn't called "fighting," or even "sparring." It is called "playing," and judo players are required to respect the rules of fair play.

Judo is not an old art. It was created in the late nineteenth century by Jigaro Kano of Tokyo, Japan, but it is based on the old combat art of jujutsu, which goes back to the sixteenth century. Jujutsu was a freewheeling, no-holds-barred kind of fighting, which stressed the importance of breaking your opponent's balance and using his force against him. Kano knew and loved jujutsu, and he intended his new system to be a refined version of it, one which would keep what was of greatest value in the older art while letting go of the techniques which were suitable only for life-and-death combat. Many of the older arts were changed in this way during the eighteenth and nineteenth centuries. The names were changed too. *Do,* meaning "the way," was either added to the end or exchanged for the traditional ending "jutsu," "the skill," "practice," or "art." All the *do* arts stressed the moral and psychological aspects of the older arts, and most of them modified or abandoned the more dangerous fighting techniques. Kano's judo emphasized the development of character as much as physical skill and focused not only on what happens in a fight but also on what happens inside you when you accept challenges and overcome fear.

When Kano established his school, the Kodokan, in Tokyo in 1886, he chose as the official insignia an eight-sided figure, because of the Japanese legend about an eight-sided mirror that was supposed to bring back light to a darkened earth. In his words, the goal of judo was "the harmonious development and perfection of human character." It was to be practiced "for the mutual welfare and benefit of all."

Judo is the most popular of all the martial arts and was the only one widely known outside of Asia before the Second World War. Theodore Roosevelt was a judo enthusiast and a judo player in 1909. Kano's school in Tokyo is still the most important school for judo players, but because Kano made his curriculum available to everyone, the system is taught and played in basically the same way all over the world.

In recent years, judo has been developed as a sport, with competitive events, records to make and break, and championships. This takes it outside the classic tradition of the *do* arts, in which the ultimate goal is an individual's self-perfection. But judo's ties to the classic tradition are honored and clear.

In 1964, men judo players were admitted to the Olympics. Women players, due largely to the work of Rusty Kanokogi, are almost sure to follow in 1988.

RUSTY
KANOKOGI

When Rusty Kanokogi first learned judo, there were no competitive judo events for women. So she competed against men, and won. Some of the first classes she taught were for men only and she made it a point to throw the largest man in the room during the first few minutes, just to "clear the air."

"I don't have to prove myself in that manner anymore," she says. "Now I play them just to keep them on their toes."

Five feet nine inches, 170 pounds, red-headed and clear-eyed, Rusty is formidable—one of the highest-ranking judo women in America, a world-class athlete, and a legend for her victories on the mat and on behalf of women in judo all over the world.

"There's no end to what judo—and all sports—can do for a person," she says. "You discover the best in yourself, the best in your competitors. It isn't fair to withhold that from someone just because she's a woman."

Rusty was born Rena Glickman in 1935 in the Coney Island section of Brooklyn. Her father died when she was very young, and her mother, an immigrant from Russia's Jewish Pale, worked hard and had very little time for Rusty or her older brother, Charles. It was her aunt, Lee Krasner, honored today as one of

America's foremost painters, who was Rusty's mentor and model.

"Aunt Lee wasn't afraid of anything," Rusty says. "She just did whatever she wanted to do, and in my book that made her Number One. She was someone I could look up to and someone I knew would always understand me."

Rusty spent as much time with her aunt as she could. But she spent most of her time on her own, out on the street, and out of her mother's way. She held almost every odd job available in Coney

Rusty throws her partner neatly to the mat with a tsuri goshi, *a "lifting, propping hip throw." Once her partner is down, she will follow through with a hold to keep him immobilized.*

Island, from peeling potatoes for the concessions on the boardwalk to selling ice water to the passengers arriving at the bus depot from New Jersey. She was a strong, energetic girl, a natural athlete at a time and in a place where there was no serious interest in sports for girls.

"Even in gym," Rusty recalls, "we never worked hard enough to break a sweat. They had us doing the Mickey-Mouse versions of everything. Nobody cared."

Outside of school, Rusty joined street games and played "as hard as the guys—harder." She played handball for hours on end, shot baskets with ease, and after watching men lift weights in a local gym, began her own weight-training program by pressing bus stop signs. With no one looking out for her, Rusty remembers feeling that she had to choose between being "a scared person" and "a strong person." Once she did, there was no stopping her. "Fighting became my sport," she says now. "It was partly survival and partly love. I was good at it."

Those were the days when every poor neighborhood sported its array of gangs, and Rusty, who would one day organize women's judo, organized the Coney Island Apaches, "the most notorious girl gang in Brooklyn," according to one reporter. The Apaches fought enthusiastically and engaged in what Rusty calls "guts training," daring one another to do dangerous things, the more daring and dangerous the better. They took turns jumping off the boardwalk onto the sand fifteen feet below. At night they crept into the abandoned buildings of burned-out Luna Amusement Park and swang from rooftop to rooftop on ropes, running from the watchman who chased after them firing a shotgun. Rusty collided with the side of a building once and ended up in Coney Island Hospital, with three ribs broken. It didn't phase her.

"Pain, getting hurt, broken bones—those were things you just had to put up with," she says. "In fact, getting hurt was glamorous—it meant you had done something dangerous. We never worried about the chances were were taking. We wanted to take chances—that was our way of having fun. I didn't go into judo for self-defense. I went into judo to calm down."

Rusty discovered judo in 1954 at the age of nineteen. Her days as an Apache were behind her. So was high school, and so was her first and "much too early" marriage. She had a newborn baby, lots of bills, and more energy than her job assisting the Physical Director of the Prospect Park YMCA could make use of. When a friend showed her what he was learning in the brand-new judo class at the Brooklyn Central Y, Rusty wanted to try judo, too.

"The class was for men only, but I got my boss at the Prospect Park Y to talk to the director at Brooklyn Central. He got permission for me to enter the class. In exchange, I was to teach whatever I learned to students at the Prospect Park Y. It was great!"

Was she a natural in judo? Far from it. In fact, judo intrigued Rusty partly because she couldn't do it.

"I thought power was power," she says, "and that's not the way judo is at all. Someone much smaller than me could just flip me right over. I couldn't figure it out. Sometimes I knew a technique was coming and still I couldn't stop it! And nobody could have been worse at forward rolls than I was. I couldn't figure out how to make my body light, how to make it fly up into the air the way they did. I had more bruises from falling the wrong way than you would believe possible. I was tall and it was a long way down!"

Rusty had to use a broom closet as a dressing room, because the Y wasn't set up to deal with women students. But the judo instructor, Al Evoy, was fair-minded and open. He took Rusty seriously and gave her a chance to work hard and show what she could do.

"I think my enthusiasm impressed him—it couldn't have been my skill," Rusty says now. "I was so grateful for the chance to learn that I put out 100 percent—no, 150 percent!"

Rusty worked with complete commitment. She never missed class, not even the night there was a snowstorm and she had to walk the four miles from her home. "All transportation had stopped," she recalls. "By the time I got to class, there was three feet of snow on the ground. Fortunately, one other lunatic showed up and we practiced together."

When the time came for Brooklyn Central to form a team, Evoy asked Rusty to be on it. "I was considered an exceptional woman," she says with a smile. "A woman who played judo like a man."

That was intended as a compliment, Rusty recalls, because everyone believed that women could not play judo. She believed it too—until she began teaching other women at the Prospect Park Y. "They worked hard. And lots of them were good. I found out that I wasn't such an exception after all. I said, 'Hey! Wait a minute! Women can so do this!' "

But the world of judo was all male, and it didn't want to hear. Rusty found out how far they would go to avoid hearing when her team entered a citywide competition organized by the Y Association under the general supervision of the Amateur Athletic Union. At that time, applications didn't say "for men only," though Rusty knew it was assumed that all players were male. She realized too that her signature, "Rusty Glickman," wouldn't make anyone think otherwise. Pushing back her short hair and staying in the middle of her teammates—who wanted her with them and insisted that she had every right to be there—Rusty entered the gym and waited for her turn on the mat. When she stepped forward, she thought she saw a few heads turn, but no one said anything. No one said anything when she won her match, either. But when she lined up with her team to get her medal, she was handed a note. The director wanted to see her.

"My teammates told me not to go," Rusty remembers. "They said, 'Stay on line and get your medal and let him stew.' But to me it was a choice between being humiliated in public and being humiliated in private. I chose privacy, so I stepped off the line."

The director was furious.

"It wasn't an athletic thing with him," Rusty says. "It wasn't that he didn't think I could do it—obviously I could! He didn't think women *should*. A woman just had no place there—and he couldn't understand how I could have thought they did."

The former Coney Island Apache did not try to defend herself. She was afraid of being expelled from the class she was in at Brooklyn Central.

"It didn't say 'male' on the application," she apologized. "If it had, I wouldn't have entered."

After that, applications from the Y Association and the AAU had the word "male" on them, and Rusty was barred from competing.

"But I could still spar during *randori*," she says, "the free sparring you do during class. No one keeps score. It's a chance to experiment, develop your moves, try out techniques, and just go. If someone had won in a competition, I would get them to spar with me during *randori*, so I had an idea of how I compared and how I would have done if I had been allowed to compete myself."

Even at that early point in her training, it was clear that Rusty was a good player. Her respect for the community of judo players—if not the rule makers—was clear, too.

"There was a kind of honor about them," Rusty says, "a sense of being on the right side. They'd fight, but they'd fight fairly. They could win or lose with the same feeling. It was a long time before I learned that. In one of my first matches, I did the most illegal thing in the world. I couldn't get my partner down no matter what techniques I used. I ended up getting so frustrated that I just muscled him down—and when he tried to get up, I kicked him in the face! I thought I was back in Coney Island, fighting in the street!"

The instructor had Rusty doing push-ups for months after that incident. "I don't think I even went home," she says. But her love for judo continued, and her loyalty was absolute.

"I was always getting injured," she remembers, "straining this, bruising that. We all were. It isn't like that anymore—but the mats we had to work on in those days were awful—they were a punishment. Once when I had to check into the emergency room because of a separated shoulder, the doctor made a face and asked me how in the world it had happened. I didn't want judo to get the blame, so I said I had fallen off a stool while I was hanging drapes."

Rusty had been training and teaching for about a year when Mamaru Saiganji, a masterful Japanese judo player who had just settled in New York, came to the Y to see the new judo class. When he set up an advanced class of his own in Manhattan, Rusty was invited to join. She was the first female student he had ever taught.

"Something seemed to click," Rusty says. "He really worked with me and for me as if he had decided to make me the best student he had ever had."

Under his instruction, Rusty came into her own as a *judoka,* a practitioner of the art and ways of judo. "He taught me as much by what he was as by what he said. He had a spirit and an attitude that made you want to be like him. He proved that the stronger you are, the less you have to carry on about it."

Mr. Saiganji helped Rusty grow both philosophically and technically. "If I couldn't get a door open," she says, "my inclination was to try to run through it. Mr. Saiganji taught me to calm down, to think, to manipulate, not to go charging in. And he helped me correct my timing, to move faster and to find better entries—the best times to move in on your partner and try to break his balance. He also taught me how to break my opponent's mind, how to break his concentration, giving myself more time for an entry and a chance for a cleaner entry."

With Mr. Saiganji, Rusty learned the technique that was to become her favorite. It is called *makikomi.* "People go to the techniques that are most natural for their bodies," she explains. "I was always broadly built, and I had strong legs. I loved *makikomi* the first time I tried it. It's a technique in which you break your

Rusty with the Judo Twins Club, where she worked with Mr. Saiganji.

opponent's balance toward you and then, for a split second you're on one leg, with your left knee slightly bent for springing. You hit the front of your opponent's thigh with the back of yours and simultaneously raise them up with your right hip. You throw them up, and you go up with them. It's a full commitment technique. You cling to your opponent and together you fly through the air, making a full circle, and come down on the mat with your body on top so that as soon as you land you are in position to immobilize them.''

Not only did Rusty's playing improve dramatically, her experience of judo and of herself as a *judoka* changed too. ''There's a time in your training when something happens to you," she says. "It isn't because someone tells you to, or even because you want it to. But you find yourself facing your partner with a kind of purity. You bow, and you begin. You have no thoughts of 'Well, I'll do this and get him or her on that.' You are pure, clean, and open, and everything good comes out of you. And 'good' fixes your speed, your timing, and your technique."

In the summer of 1961, as one of Mr. Saiganji's advanced students, Rusty participated in an international meet held aboard *HMS Queen Elizabeth* in New York harbor. British women had been playing high-level judo for years and were allowed to enter competitions, so Rusty's presence on the American team was not a problem. It was unusual, however, because British women were usually matched against other women. Rusty was to play a man.

"I won my match," Rusty remembers, "and that gave our team the winning point. It was wonderful! The whole team loved me, and articles were written about me in British newspapers. They called me this 'great American woman' and thought my beating the British man was a big event. It was incredible!"

Several European magazines reprinted the article, and Rusty began to get letters from people in many different countries, including one from a woman in Australia named Pat Strange. "It turned out that women judo players in Australia were already so organized that several high-level national competitions had been held—while in America we were not even recognized. Pat and I started to correspond, and she gave me lots of pointers on how to go about getting women's judo off the ground in America. Other women wrote too. We began to have a network of women judo players—a worldwide network. I didn't have any money or I would have gone all over the world and played everybody."

Women in the United States wrote to Rusty, too. One, Phyllis Harper from Chicago, had been training in judo almost as long as

Rusty had. She also had been teaching women. Rusty and Phyllis became allies in the fight to bring recognition to women's judo in America.

In June, 1962, Rusty was promoted to black belt. The next month she was on a plane bound for Japan to study in the Kodokan. She arrived, she says with a laugh, "like Paddington," with a letter of introduction from Mr. Saiganji in one hand and a set of luggage given to her by her students in the other. It was to be the most extraordinary summer of her life.

Rusty checked into the women's training hall, as she was supposed to.

"It wasn't what I wanted," she says. "Mr. Saiganji had told me they would not be playing the kind of judo I played. Japanese women were taught a much more refined, milder form. But he said I could learn a lot about technique from them, and besides I didn't have any choice. At the Kodokan, women trained in their own separate area, and that was that. Still, it was the Kodokan, and I was happy to be there."

Each day, senior instructors toured all the training halls, observing the students and the exercises. Occasionally, they joined the students in *randori*. "When they played with me," Rusty recalls, "I really opened up. They always won, but I got some good moves in."

Soon she was invited to play in the "foreign dojo," a small training hall for *judoka* from other countries. There were twelve other players working there, all of them men. "They were not delighted to see me," Rusty says. "I guess they thought I would bring down the level of their play."

A few days after she began to work in the foreign dojo, a messenger from the main dojo, which was for men only, entered the room and motioned her to follow him. "I thought, 'Uh oh! I must have done something wrong.' I bowed off the mat and followed him. He didn't say a word."

Rusty immobilizes her partner with a kesa-gatame, *a "scarf hold," so called because in it you wrap your arm around your partner's neck like a scarf.*

Randori was going on in the main training hall when Rusty entered. She stood on the side, near the instructors who were observing the students. One of the instructors noticed her and pointed to the mat.

"Please, please," he said.

Rusty stepped onto the mat. Another player bowed and came toward her.

"I realized that the instructors wanted to see what I could do," Rusty says. "I bowed, and we began. I threw him as fast as I could, and I just kept going. Two seconds didn't pass without my doing an attack. I played like I was playing for my life. Then the command came to stop. We bowed, and that was that. Another player came over, we bowed, and did it all again. Most of the players there were much better than I was and they had no mercy. It was incredible. It was judo the way I had always dreamed it."

After that day, Rusty checked into the women's dojo every morning, out of respect for the class. But she trained in the main dojo. She is the only woman ever invited to do so.

"We were there nine hours a day," she says, "every day. I thought I had died and gone to heaven."

Instructors from all over Japan—"fourth-degree black belts and up"—were her instructors. She learned throws and pinning techniques she had never seen before. Her timing improved, her use of muscular power diminished, she began to feel as though she could stay in the air forever if she needed to.

"When it's something you love, you can do it as long as your body holds out. After a while you feel as though you are walking on air. You are clean inside, you are pure and happy. You don't want to fight the world. You don't have any anger in you at all. You are satisfied."

TV cameras came to film "the American mother" training in the main dojo. Journalists came to interview her. One Kodokan elder, a man who had been the All-Japan Judo Champion in 1938 and traveled down to the Kodokan from the mountains on horseback, took it upon himself to become Rusty's sponsor. He never spoke to her, but he gave money to the teachers with instructions that it be given to "the American woman." If he saw her in the Kodokan restaurant, he'd signal to the waiter and order a full-course meal for her. Another elder sent a chauffeur for Rusty with instructions to take her any place she wanted to go. World-famous teachers, people Rusty had only read about in books, asked to meet with her and gave her pointers to help her improve her judo. And a few days before the end of the summer, Rusty was asked to take the test for second-degree black belt.

"I thought it was a mistake," she says, "because I had only gotten my first degree two months before."

Risei Kano, president of the Kodokan and son of Jigaro Kano himself, came to observe Rusty's test. "It was like performing before the president of the United States. I thought people could hear my heart beating all the way back in Brooklyn."

The first part of the test was *randori*. Rusty had to play three matches against three different players assigned to her for the test. Each match lasted three minutes. Then with another partner assigned to her, she had to perform a *kata* called *nage-no-kata*. It consisted of fifteen formal throwing techniques. She performed the *kata* twice—first as the thrower and then as the faller. Finally was *katame-no-kata*, fifteen formal mat techniques. Rusty had to execute five immobilizations, five chokes, and five arm bars.

In spite of her nerves, her performance was excellent and she was honorably promoted. Three days later, September 4, 1962, she left Japan for America, loaded with almost two hundred gifts— fans, combs, books, dolls, scarves, rings, pictures, placques, and bells from her teachers and her fellow students. Rusty was enor-

This choke is called a kata juji jime, *an "over-the-shoulder choke." Your partner may end the choke by tapping the mat. If he doesn't, you may continue until he passes out.*

mously well liked and everyone wanted to wish her well. Among the friends she made was a young man named Ryohei Kanokogi, a champion judo player from Kyushu Province, who was thinking of coming to America to live when he finished his studies at Nihon University.

"The officials at customs thought I was looting Japan," Rusty laughs. "There were presents everywhere."

In New York, Rusty's students met her at the airport. Her son Chris, who had spent the summer with his grandparents, was waiting for her at home. So were offers to teach judo (to men!) at three New York schools. Rusty was flying, "thrilled and re-thrilled," she says. Everything seemed to be working for her.

And yet, Rusty was nothing if not a realist. She could not ignore the fact that certain things remained unchanged. She had been honored as an exceptional woman, but men were still the "real" judo players. Some of the rules had been broken for her, but they were still the rules. Being treated as an exception did not make things right. In fact, it was harmful, because it confirmed the impression that most women—"normal" women—didn't have what it takes to be good at judo and didn't deserve a full place in it.

Rusty continued to teach and to train. But she committed herself to a larger goal, to changing the beliefs and the rules of the judo community, to making a real place in it for women. It would prove to be a surprisingly difficult struggle, one which would last more than twenty years.

In the spring of 1963, Ryohei Kanokogi, the young man from Kyushu Province, came to New York to live. A year later, he and Rusty were married. Today, they run the Kyushu Judo School in Brooklyn. With Ryohei a sixth-degree black belt, and Rusty a fourth-degree, they are the highest-ranking judo couple in America, perhaps in the world. In addition to Chris they have a daughter, Jean, born in 1966 (in 1982 she was a National High School Judo Champion), and a son Teddy, born in 1970.

"Ryohei is a champion judo player," Rusty says proudly, "and a champion supporter of women in judo. He has been for us right from the start."

In 1970, with the women's movement beginning to make itself felt, and Rusty campaigning behind the scenes for the rights of women in judo, the AAU, which had kept Rusty's medal from her in 1961 because it did not believe women should compete—finally agreed to allow women in competitions. But the AAU said women would have to spar according to certain "women's rules." When Rusty saw the rules, she didn't know whether to laugh or cry.

"Judo is a contact sport, but the AAU wanted women to have as little contact as possible. I guess they thought it wasn't ladylike. They practically eliminated matwork, modified almost every technique, and they completely outlawed my favorite—*makikomi!* They said, 'No! No! That's not nice! Women shouldn't do that!' I think they thought we would catch on fire!"

Rusty organized opposition to the rules. It took three years, but in 1973, the AAU came around. There were no longer women's rules and men's rules. There were only the rules of judo, and they were the same for everyone. The first AAU national competition for women was scheduled to take place in November, 1974, in Phoenix. It was about time.

Strictly speaking, Rusty was not eligible for the AAU nationals since teachers are not considered "amateurs." And she certainly didn't have to compete in order to prove her skill. But she entered the event anyway.

"I wanted my name on the record," she says. "I had worked so hard for this, and I wanted to be in it! The first national competition for women in judo ever held in the United States."

Rusty qualified to compete in the 165-pound-and-under division, even though that is slightly lower than her natural weight. Her good friend and protege Maureen Braziel was entering the over-165 division, and Rusty didn't want to compete against her.

Rusty helps Maureen Braziel perfect the kata guruma *("shoulder-wheel") throw. Maureen must continue the wheel form, pulling with her left hand, until a complete circle has been made and her partner has been dropped to the mat.*

She dieted carefully before the nationals and, according to her scale, was down to a safe 164 on the morning of the flight to Phoenix. But the scale out there read 171. She couldn't understand it, and neither could her friends. It is common for scales to vary by a few pounds—but not by seven. Still, there was no arguing with it. She decided to steam the weight off, a common practice among athletes who need to lose a pound or two in order to qualify. Seven pounds was a lot more than usual, but Rusty was sure she could handle it.

In the bathroom of her hotel suite, with the hot water running full force, she jogged in place for four hours, stopping at intervals only to be weighed. By the end of that time, her friends had to help her walk, and her fair skin had a purplish cast to it, but she weighed in at 164. Her event was scheduled for the next day.

Rusty suffered from severe cramps and nausea all night long. In the morning, when she was called to the mat for her match, everything looked "dreamy," and she realized she couldn't close her hands to grip. She stood there wondering what was wrong.

Down on the mat, Rusty began to cough up blood. She tapped the ground as a signal for her opponent to release her hold. Then the referee was beside her with a towel. Rusty could not speak. The match was over.

Doctors told her later that she had lost so much potassium during her marathon steaming that she should have had a heart attack right then and there. She was lucky to have survived.

The weeks that followed were the worst of Rusty's life. "I knew there were medical reasons for what happened, but I felt as though my judo should have come through for me anyway. I thought I was just no good, and I wondered whether I ever had been."

It took months for Rusty to struggle back to health, and to shed the confusion about herself and her skills that the episode had caused her. But when she looks back on it now, she isn't sorry that she entered, or that things turned out the way they did. "It made me realize that I had to choose. I could either go into training and be a serious competitor myself or be a coach and teacher, and help other people to move ahead. Both those things take 100 percent of your energy, so you really have to choose between them. At thirty-seven, with three children—two of them still young—and a near disaster behind me, it was easy to choose."

After that, things began to move quickly. The number of good judo women at the first national in Phoenix convinced Rusty that the United States should have a women's team. She got the AAU to set one up, and in 1976, she accompanied it, as coach, to the' British Women's Judo Open, an international event that attracted the best women players in the world. Maureen Braziel won the gold medal, the first time it had been taken away from England.

Between matches, Rusty and Maureen discuss technique.

The number of good judo women at the British Open convinced Rusty that women judo players should be in the Olympics. For that, women's judo would have to become an official "world sport." There would have to be a Women's World Judo Championship and women from at least three continents would have to participate. Rusty took the project on, the biggest single project she had ever undertaken.

She was hard at work on it when a crisis developed in another quarter—the Maccabiah Games, an international competition for Jewish athletes begun in 1937, when Jews were barred from the Olympics. The Israelis wanted to include women judo players in the 1977 Games and had asked the American Sports for Israel Committee to draw up a list of top Jewish women players. But the chairman of the committee had ignored the request.

Rusty found out, and decided it was worth fighting. Plotting strategy with judo friends in Europe and with the Maccabiah organizers in Israel, she assembled a team on her own. The chairman of the American Sports for Israel Committee resisted to the end, but when Rusty threatened a court injunction, which would stop all Americans in all the sports from going to Israel, he conceded. The American women judo players went. They won medals for the United States, but much more important, they won respect for the rights of women athletes everywhere.

For a while after that, Rusty was a one-woman international action committee. She kept a watch on events all over the world. If American athletes were participating, she wanted to know whether women were among them. If they were not, she took action. Sometimes this involved hiring a lawyer and threatening a lawsuit. But Rusty knew enough about the law by then to do most of the legal maneuvering herself.

Her priority was always judo, but she was willing to lend her energy in every case in which women seemed to be discriminated against. "It's not just judo," she says. "It isn't even just sports. It's life."

In 1980, three years after she began work on it, the First Women's World Judo Championships were held in Madison Square Garden. The two-day event cost $180,000. It drew 150 women from twenty-seven countries and five continents, and it established women's judo as a sport of Olympic stature. As Tournament Director and President of the Organizing Committee, Rusty was honored by the White House, the Governor of New York, the Mayor of New York City, and the President of the International Judo Federation.

There is still a lot to do. Women's place in judo and in the Olympics is not yet guaranteed. Rusty herself, due to be promoted to fifth-degree black belt—a level achieved by very few people in the world, male or female—may have to fight for her rank against an old rule that discriminates against women and stipulates that fifteen years must pass before women above fourth degree can be promoted to a higher rank. But the woman who used to jump from the boardwalk on a dare has never turned her back on a fight yet. If she has to fight again, she will. Rusty Kanokogi has never asked that things be easy, but she insists that they be fair.

Karate

KARATE IS THE SYSTEM OF EMPTY-HANDED FIGHTING THAT STRESSES FO-
cus, concentration, and the proper use of technique to create an
extraordinary skill in the people who learn it. You use hands, feet,
arms, and legs as weapons and shields. You learn stances and
postures that root you to the ground so that your strikes and blocks
are solid. You learn *katas*—sets of movements which are formal,
precise, and as beautiful as dances—in which you match yourself
against imaginary opponents. You do endurance exercises,
stretching exercises, strengthening exercises. But the kind of fighting power possessed by the best *karateka*, practitioners of the art, is
not the result of muscular power alone. Karate calls upon and seeks
to strengthen the will as well as the body. It teaches an attitude of
determination, a readiness to stand up to challenges. And it
teaches you to summon up and use your inner energy, your *ki*.

You can see this at work most clearly in the *kiai*, the shout which
sometimes accompanies a strike. Although a ferocious shout can
frighten an opponent and is a good technique in itself, a *kiai* is
more than a shout. The word means a gathering or harmonizing or
bringing together (*ai*) of spiritual or internal energy (*ki*). A *kiai* is a
way of summoning your inner power. With a *kiai*, your strike feels
like a burst of focused energy that comes from the center of your
being, and that is exactly what a karate strike is supposed to be. The

46

strike has been used to break boards, bricks, and stones—feats that are clearly not the result of strength alone, but of technique. The *kiai* is at the heart of it. Although in beginners it may be just a shout, masters have been known to *kiai* without making a sound.

Karate began in the fifteenth century on the island of Okinawa, then an independent state. It was called *Okinawa-te,* which means "Okinawa-hands," and sometimes *Kara-te,* which means "China-hands," in recognition of the Chinese systems that were its inspiration. Although empty-handed fighting styles based on Chinese systems were known in Okinawa as early as the eighth century, it wasn't until the fifteenth century, when the king banned swords and other weapons that might be used against his soldiers, that Okinawan empty-handed fighting developed into something distinctive. In the seventeenth century, when the Japanese occupied Okinawa and banned not only weapons but empty-handed fighting, too, it went underground. Practiced in secret by farmers and peasants who wished to defend themselves and resist the Japanese, it blossomed into a full-fledged art.

Karate spread to Japan early in the twentieth century when Gichin Funakoshi, one of the great Okinawan masters, set up a school, the Shotokan, in Tokyo. By the 1930s, karate was popular all over Japan. New movements and styles began to be seen, and the name was changed. The character that means "Chinese" was replaced by the one that means "empty." (Both characters are pronounced *kara,* so the change doesn't register in English at all.)

After the Second World War, karate became popular throughout the world as a sport—with tournaments that featured competitive matches and karate associations that honored champions and kept track of records. But it has also maintained its identity as a people's art and has had a special appeal among groups who are out of power and who are working for social and civil change—Third World people, people in the underclasses of society, and most recently, women. Annie Ellman is part of this tradition.

ANNIE ELLMAN

T he martial arts combine elements I cannot live without," says Annie Ellman, a small (barely five feet), soft-spoken woman who has a warm smile, a thoughtful air, and a third-degree black belt in *goju* karate. "They teach us about harmony, living with respect for nature, and they help us develop the fighting spirit we need to resist the wrongs of this world."

Annie is a founder and the chief instructor of Brooklyn Women's Martial Arts, one of the oldest and largest karate schools for women in the United States. She has worked with hundreds of women since the school began, but most of them don't know what her rank is. Annie doesn't wear a belt. She doesn't believe in belts, ranks, titles, or competition. Instead, she urges each student to make her own best effort, to keep working even when she feels discouraged, and never to say "I can't."

"Women are constantly being told we can't do things, or that we'll never be able to do them well," Annie says. "At BWMA we ask students to stop believing all the negative things they've been told about themselves. We want them to break out of the patterns of self-doubt and passivity, which only serve to keep them down."

Most of the things Annie talks to her students about are things she has experienced herself. "I know how hard it is to believe in

49

Annie works on a double strike to the face and groin, the final move of the ten-point blocking system. Ten-point, a soft system, uses circular moves and gains its power from ki *rather than muscular development. As such it is unique to the* goju *(go—hard, ju—soft) style of karate Annie practices.*

what you're doing," she says, "and to believe in yourself. I've been teaching karate for almost ten years, but there are still times when I feel like I don't belong here, and I wonder: What am I doing teaching women how to fight?"

Annie doesn't think of herself as a fighter. But in some ways, she has always been one. Raised in a lakeside community north of New York City, she was a crackerjack student, an exuberant natural athlete, and a thoughtful girl who spent hours watching the wind on the lake and the patterns of leaves as they fell. People who knew her then described her as bubbly and bright and full of good spirits—but there was another side to Annie. In the fall of 1957, soon after Annie's seventh birthday, it was discovered that she had epilepsy, a disorder of the brain that makes people subject to seizures, sudden, uncontrollable losses of consciousness during which the body becomes rigid and may go into spasms. Victims are totally exhausted for hours after a seizure and may suffer from violent headaches. Growing up became a struggle and a fight for Annie.

"Going into a seizure was terrifying," she says. "I'd feel like I was draining away, watching myself die. And my mother told me never to tell anyone. She said people wouldn't understand and that it would have to be a secret."

Annie's parents wanted to protect her from the stigma attached to epilepsy in those days. Even the family doctor advised them not to notify Annie's school about her illness, partly because it might "keep her out of things" and partly because people would be alarmed and view her with apprehension if they knew. Since it was a disorder of the brain, epilepsy was sometimes thought to be a form of insanity or retardation. The seizures made epileptics seem all the more strange and discomfiting.

"I didn't tell anyone," Annie says, "but I was still frightened. I ended up running away from myself and turning my back on the things I was feeling, as if I were two people, one who had epilepsy and one who didn't."

Because seizures were so frightening and so unpredictable, Annie felt uneasy about being alone. Though she felt isolated when she was with other people, because she was hiding such an important part of herself, she came to shun solitude entirely and turned away even from individual sports. "Except for swimming and ice-skating, which I already knew and loved, the only sports I would do were team sports. I hated gymnastics, even though I was good at it, and I hated running. I just didn't want to be alone."

The turmoil Annie experienced during those years was entirely hidden from outsiders. In spite of her illness, or because of it, she was a very hard worker and excelled in almost everything she did. An all-around athlete and a straight-A student, she was secretary of her high school honor society, secretary and vice-president of the student government. At sixteen, she was selected by the American Field Service Committee to go to Iran as a summer exchange student. Annie kept her epilepsy secret from the officials in charge and from the Iranian family with whom she lived for the two months she was there.

Outside of school, Annie worked as a volunteer aide in a nursing home, a big sister in a Harlem youth project, a tutor in a local elementary school. Sometimes she worked with her sister Linda, three years older.

"Linda and I were raised to believe that when things are wrong, you do something. We weren't given directives or told to go out and get involved. But issues were always being discussed in our home, people were always making plans and organizing things, and we became activists more or less by osmosis."

Annie's mother, a long-time member of Women Strike for Peace, took Annie on her first peace march when she was ten. Annie's grandmother Alta had been a radical and an activist since her youth in pre-Revolutionary Russia where, one of her brothers later wrote, she "challenged the Tsar's gendarmes" and met in secret to organize the peasants against them. Arriving in America at the age of nineteen, the oldest of eight children, Alta went to work as a finisher in the garment industry of New York and helped to unionize the women in the sweatshops there. Later, she named her firstborn daughter, Nora, after the heroine in Henrik Ibsen's play *A Doll's House*, who resisted the demands of her culture and left her home to become a "free woman."

"My mother used to say that while others might make sandwiches for the revolution," Annie remembers, "Alta would make the revolution."

In 1968, Annie finished high school—eighth in a class of 205— and entered the College of Old Westbury, a new, experimental branch of the State University of New York. Students were to have an equal voice with faculty members in all matters that affected

Three moves from kata seisan, *demonstrating the hard and soft interpretations characteristic of goju.* above: *a long, low stance is accompanied by open-handed blocks and strikes;* below left: *the "cat" stance, designed to cover distance and surprise one's attacker with a kick from the front leg;* below right: *a turn completed, sinking into the lowest of the three postures, with close-fisted hard blocks.*

them and courses were designed to be relevant to the affairs of the world. Annie's mother had found the school and encouraged Annie to go there.

"My sister had gone to the University of Chicago and was so involved in the student protests there that it looked as if she might be expelled at any minute. My mother wanted me closer to home and in a school which was not authoritarian, where I would be allowed to be active and involved if I wanted to be."

Old Westbury filled the bill. Annie had no sooner arrived on campus than she was propelled into the thick of the highly controversial New York City teacher's strike, a strike filled with tension and charges of racial bigotry. Teachers and the board of education were pitted against the parents in Harlem, Bedford-Stuyvesant, and other black communities, who wanted more control over the schools their children attended. When the teachers' union called a strike, parents and community leaders appealed for volunteers to help them keep the schools open. Annie and other Old Westbury students were excused from classes so they could pitch in.

Later that year Annie worked, for college credit, with children in the mental health clinic of a central Brooklyn hospital. The next year, she joined the first women's group ever established at Old Westbury, launched in part by friends of her sister, who had enrolled there when they were expelled from the University of Chicago. Annie discovered how much she shared with other women as the group explored attitudes and ideas, experiences and feelings. Later she joined a panel of women who visited local high schools to talk about the new women's movement and to explain the issues involved—although at first, Annie recalls, she was "too tongue-tied to say a word."

Toward the end of the year, she demonstrated with the Young Lords, a radical Puerto Rican group that had members among Old Westbury students. They occupied a church on the edge of Harlem for nearly a week. The organizers brought in food and supplies. Annie's mother brought her a supply of epilepsy medicine, secretly passing it to her through an open window when no one was nearby.

Old Westbury was certainly not an ivory tower and the students there were anything but sheltered. But even Old Westbury wasn't the real world. And by the end of Annie's sophomore year, nothing less than the real world would do. In June of 1970, she quit school and headed west. It was in Berkeley, in what people called "the liberated zone," that she discovered karate.

"It was in the air," Annie says. "It was part of the culture then, the culture of change and resistance. We wanted to change society and we wanted to change ourselves and create what we called the new human being, the new woman and the new man."

Karate fit right into this context and basic courses for women were springing up all over Berkeley. Annie enrolled in her first course in the fall of 1970. "I loved it from the very first minute. I felt aware of my body in a whole new way and I felt stronger and more alive than I had ever felt before."

Her greatest asset when she began was her energy. "I wasn't particularly strong or limber," she says, "but I could move. I was well coordinated. And I had energy, and I think that was the main thing. Martial artists have to be able to get their energy up. And I could do that in karate, even though I was on barbiturates. I was able to get my energy going. The release, the joy I felt was just incredible. It was more exhilarating than anything I had ever done before. I felt as though I was discovering a whole new world and a whole new way of being."

Inspired by karate and by the ideal of the new woman, Annie joined the activities of the Berkeley women's community, one of the most active centers of the women's movement in America. "We wanted equality and beyond," Annie says. "We wanted physical strength, practical skills, independence—all the things we missed

During free-sparring, Annie, who likes to use close-in techniques, rushes to a flying knee charge.

because we had been told they were beyond us."

A top priority in those days was acquiring the skills needed for self-reliance. Annie joined several workshops—including one in basic carpentry and another in automobile mechanics—along with scores of other women. But for her, self-reliance came to mean, in addition, dealing with epilepsy. She was able to tell people about it by this time, although she recalls that first saying the word out loud had been "the hardest thing I ever did in my life."

She had had a particularly severe seizure a few months after arriving in California, and the strength of her medication had been greatly increased. Waking up in the morning had become a struggle, and although in karate she felt strong and in control of her energy, she was sometimes drowsy during the rest of the day. Then she learned that in addition to everything else, the medication she was taking might prevent her from ever having children.

"It all seemed so wrong," she says. "The side effects, the consequences no one had ever told me about, the fact that I had no control, no influence over what was happening to me or what might happen in the future."

Returning east, Annie broached the subject of drug-dependence and barbiturates with her family, hoping that they would understand her need to look for an alternative. Though they were frightened for her, and believed that there was no alternative, they helped her investigate non-traditional approaches and methods of treatment. When a family friend recommended a homeopathic doctor, Annie went to see him.

"He explained the belief of homeopathic medicine that the body can cure itself," Annie recalls, "and that outside preparations can help by enhancing the body's own healing powers. Drugs, especially barbiturates, he considered poisons."

Annie was put on a "detoxification" regimen and given homeopathic remedies designed to help her body defend itself from seizures. "For the first time in almost my entire life, I was free of drugs. I've been free ever since."

Annie has had very few seizures in the years since then, and the seizures she has had have been very mild. Epilepsy sometimes becomes milder in adulthood, and that may be what happened in Annie's case. But she also credits the homeopathic regimen and is a wholehearted champion of the homeopathic approach to illness and health.

Back in California, Annie continued to train in karate, loving it more than ever. For the next few years, however, her training was sporadic. She traveled often between California and New York. She tried to find classes wherever she went, and she developed considerable skill. But she did not have any serious ambitions in it.

"I felt the way I would have felt if I'd been introduced to Chinese calligraphy," she says. "I thought it was wonderful, and I loved to do it, but I didn't think I'd ever develop any real proficiency."

Her first concern throughout these years was to find political work she could put her heart into. In California, she worked with a myriad of collectives, women's groups, Third World groups, anti-war groups. In New York she worked mostly with a neighborhood organization called Homefront, which rallied people against the Vietnam War and on behalf of a score of issues facing them "at home," from racism to homosexual rights, police brutality to women's liberation.

Annie's sister, who had settled in Brooklyn, worked with Homefront too. When Annie was in New York, she and Linda worked together. They leafletted the neighborhood, set up meetings, clothing exchange depots, workshops for women on everything from automobile repair to household wiring. They worked on the mammoth "people's festival" in Brooklyn's Prospect Park to celebrate the signing of the "people's peace treaty between the people of the United States and the people of Vietnam."

At an anti-war demonstration in New York City, where Annie finally settled in 1973, she met Nadia Telsey and began to tie together her love for karate and her commitment to social change.

Nadia was teaching a women's class at a karate school in Manhattan called the Temple for Physical and Spiritual Survival. She was also training there with founder and chief instructor Gerald Orange, one of the few martial artists in New York who made women feel welcome in his school and hopeful about their potential as artists and fighters. Annie enrolled in Nadia's class, and found in her a model, then a partner, then a lifetime friend.

"Nadia was already working with other women in the Women's Martial Arts Union and doing demonstrations when I met her, and she knew how to present the martial arts in a political way. She was a wonderful organizer and she really knew how to get things out there."

They began to work on projects together, both of them "constantly juggling" their schedules between work, meetings and classes. "We were always leaving something a little early to get to something else a little late."

In Gerald Orange, Annie found a source of enlightenment about the meaning of the martial arts, and a teacher whose energy and compassion seemed boundless.

"Gerald was an inspirational teacher," Annie says. "He understood oppression because of his own experiences as a black, and he saw the connection between self-defense and the quality of a person's spirit. For him, the martial arts were a way to gain spiritual strength—self-respect and self-love. They were about taking control over what you become in this world, becoming active, molding yourself instead of being molded."

At Gerald's school, Annie trained consistently, sometimes daily, and she was soon among the most advanced students.

"As a beginner, things often came easily to me," Annie says. "And they did in karate too. But above a certain level, I don't think it's easy for anyone. I had to work very hard, and I didn't always succeed. I couldn't get the back kick for months. It felt completely unnatural to me. I couldn't get my foot position right, and I was

Annie (center), *Nadia Telsey* (right), *and student Robin Lane perform* kata *to music at a street fair in Brooklyn in 1978. Annie believes public demonstrations are excellent ways to educate people about karate and "a different part of womanhood."*

always hitting with my toes instead of my heel. Gerald and Nadia both worked with me. Nadia even had a dream in which I finally got it right."

From the beginning, Annie had preferred sparring to *kata*, the sets of movements—strikes, blocks, stances, advances, and turns—that contain the essence of the style and the art.

"*Kata* is done alone," she explains. "It's just you and an imaginary enemy moving across the floor. I didn't like the starkness, the isolation of it. But I always liked to spar. I liked that back and forth flow of movement and skill and energy between two people."

Sparring, too, had been easy in the beginning. But at higher levels, Annie was often dissatisfied and impatient with herself. After one match in which she was kicked hard in the face, she left the floor furious with herself and ready to give up. "Much worse than the fact that I was hurt was that I felt like a fool," she says. "I felt like I was just no good."

Gerald agreed that Annie should have been able to block that kick, but he would not let her quit. Instead, he sparred with her himself, insisting that she had better blocks and timing in her, and that she let her real skills come out. "Gerald wouldn't let anyone quit. He wouldn't accept failure. His roots were in the evangelical church and he just wouldn't take no for an answer."

Working with Gerald and Nadia, Annie's belief in the value of karate and what it had to offer women deepened. In a world filled with violence, where women seemed "primarily victims," training in a martial art seemed a political act, an act of resistance to the way things were, and an act of faith in the possibility of change.

"I love karate," Annie says now. "And I think it's beautiful as an art. But it's much more than that. If it wasn't, I couldn't do it."

In the spring of 1974, Annie and Nadia gave a karate demonstration for women at a community center in Brooklyn. They performed *katas* together, demonstrated basic front punches and front kicks, and showed the audience the most vulnerable spots on the

In boonkai, *a* kata *is performed against a real opponent. All the moves, strikes, blocks, and sweeps are pre-arranged, but the action is fast and it looks and feels like a real match. Here Annie takes down partner Mary Wexford, holding her with her left hand and sweeping her with her left foot. Annie's* kiai *is part of the* kata.

human body, the places at which to aim when you must defend yourself from attack. Throughout the demonstration, they stressed the fact that all women could acquire self-defense and fighting skills. Afterwards, they were flooded with requests for a full-fledged class.

Nadia, still teaching at Gerald's school, couldn't do it. "I didn't want to do it alone," Annie says, "but I couldn't get anybody to do it with me."

Annie turned out to be a patient, intuitive teacher, concerned about her students' struggles, able to inspire them by her own commitment and her own example.

"There is so much for women to overcome when they begin a martial art," she says. "It goes against the grain of almost everything we've ever been taught. From the beginning we held meetings after class—in fact, pot-luck dinners were our first formal structures—so we would have a chance to talk about our feelings and the things we were going through."

Belts, ranks, and championships were far from Annie's mind. "I wanted it to be clear from the start that we weren't out to compete with one another. The martial arts were for all of us, not just the gifted ones. We were changing the habits and attitudes of a lifetime and doing things everyone said we couldn't do, and we needed one another's help along the way. I used to say that we were all going to get strong together and that we weren't going to leave anybody behind."

In the winter, Nadia ended her class at Gerald's school, and Annie persuaded her to come to Brooklyn. Together they founded Brooklyn Women's Martial Arts. At first the name was the most stable thing about it.

"We didn't have our own space, and for a while it didn't look as though we ever would. There was a lot of apprehension then about women's karate classes—people weren't sure they were in favor of them. We rented space wherever we could—sometimes by the

Annie shows the students in her children's class the proper leg position for a front kick.

class. When we had no other place, we trained in the park. Sometimes I taught in my living room."

In the spring of 1977, Annie found the loft that has become the school's permanent home. Brooklyn Women's Martial Arts has grown a great deal since then, and students now come from all over the metropolitan area. But it has remained a neighborhood school, working with and sharing its resources with other community groups. And it has remained a school that believes that all women can benefit from training in karate and that all women have the right to learn self-defense. "Many schools talk about a non-competitive, supportive approach, but this one really achieves it," said a glowing description of BWMA in a *New York Magazine* feature about self-defense instruction in New York City.

The self-defense courses given at the school are, whenever possible, free. Annie considers them a top priority. "Because of the amount of time involved, most women will not be able to train in karate. But every single woman can learn how to defend herself. And with the amount of violence against women that exists in our culture, every woman should. That's the answer I come up with when I begin to doubt myself and what I am doing with my life. Why am I teaching women how to fight? Because we need to become strong. We need to see ourselves change. When we change, we know everyone can. Then we know the world can change. And that's really what it's all about. The struggle of women in our time is a collective struggle." She ends her classes with all the students in a circle, bowing in courtesy "to each other, to our strength."

Through karate Annie has come to terms with solitude, too. "Karate supported my independence," she says. "It is the way I found to go inside myself and to come out of myself. I feel it most in *kata*, because that's the part in which you are most alone, and it's the part I didn't like at all when I began. It feels entirely different to me now. It is an unfolding of myself, something that makes me stronger and more in harmony with life. I do *kata* alone for hours now, especially when I'm feeling really distressed, and when I do I feel my energy building and going forth. I think the things karate has to give people are endless."

In 1980, Nadia left Brooklyn for Oregon, where she lives today, working and training in kung fu. She and Annie are still the best of friends, writing often and visiting when they can. Annie herself is a mother now. Her daughter, Tanya, was born in January, 1979. "Having a baby made me reevaluate my commitment to the martial arts, since I was forced to continually balance my time and my energy. But in the end my commitment has deepened. Tanya has taught me a lot about human potential and the incredible power of human life."

Last year, on International Women's Day, Annie asked her students to think of a woman who had been an inspiration to them. Then she asked each student to step forward and dedicate something she had learned in karate to that woman. Beginning students could do a single punch if they wished. One woman simply bowed. Then it was Annie's turn.

"I dedicate this to my grandmother Alta," she said, "a strong woman of her time, a fighter, and a revolutionary. When she was old, her eyesight failed and I used to read to her. She always wanted to know what was going on in the world, and she always said she hoped I would follow in her footsteps."

Kung Fu

KUNG FU IS NOT THE NAME OF AN INDIVIDUAL MARTIAL ART. IT IS A CHI-
nese phrase which means "task," "physical exercise," or "something that takes a long time to accomplish." Outside of China, it is
used to refer to the Chinese martial arts as a group. (In China itself,
the phrase for the martial arts is *wu su*.) Any one of hundreds of
systems and styles might be taught in a school of kung fu, although
some, like t'ai chi ch'uan, are so distinctive and popular that they
are usually listed separately and taught in schools that bear their
name.

The systems and styles that make up kung fu are commonly
divided into two categories: external, or hard, and internal, or
soft. The division is not absolute, and most systems and styles
contain elements of both. In general, systems are considered external if they stress muscular strength, speed, straight-line
techniques, leaps, and other calisthenic-like movements. Internal
systems tend to minimize the importance of muscular strength and
stress instead the development of inner energy, *ch'i*, (the *ki* of the
Japanese arts). Often compared to electricity, *ch'i* itself cannot be
seen. It is vital energy, the source of movement in living things,
often identified with the essence of life itself. At advanced levels,
all kung fu systems, external as well as internal, teach practitioners

to gather, develop, and use *ch'i.* But internal systems concentrate on it from the very beginning, often to the exclusion of muscular strength. Movements tend to be slower, smoother, less acrobatic, and more dancelike.

The Chinese martial arts were the first to develop. Most of them, at advanced levels, include weapons. Some weapons—spears and swords for example—are traditional. Others—pitchforks and fishing nets—developed from the tools and implements people used in daily life. All weapons are considered extensions of the body. Practitioners learn to feel as connected to their weapons as they do to their hands and feet.

Kung fu training has always included instruction in health care, nutrition, and healing. In addition to physical exercises and breathing techniques designed to promote inner and outer strength and fitness, students routinely learned to make ointments and therapeutic herbal drinks, to set broken bones, to treat open wounds, sprains, and bruises. Kung fu masters were often full-fledged physicians. All practitioners knew a great deal about how to strengthen the body and maintain its good health.

Respect for nature has always been an important part of the Chinese martial spirit. The greatest inspiration for this has been Taosim, a system of thought which dates from the fifth century B.C.E. Taoism stresses our bonds with nature and the harmony that exists between everything in the universe. Most kung fu systems try to help us experience our connections to the natural world and the forces of nature by means of meditative techniques and special exercises. Many styles are modeled on the movements of wild animals, like the leopard, the tiger, and the bear. There is even a praying mantis system.

Taoism also stresses the strength of things that are flexible and soft—like the willow tree, which survives the storm because it can bend in the wind. This idea has many fighting applications and is central to the soft, internal kung fu systems like t'ai chi ch-uan, the subject of a separate chapter.

Throughout its history in China, kung fu training was not available to the general public. At first it was contained within Buddhist communities. But even as it became known to the outside world, it was practiced and taught in secret and passed on only to carefully selected students. The powers of the arts were considered too dangerous for just anyone to learn or even to know about. Individual masters might teach only those who came from a particular village or region, family or clan.

In the twentieth century, some kung fu masters opened schools in the United States, but until the 1960s, they accepted only students of Chinese descent. The handful of other Americans—if there were that many—who knew anything about kung fu were the ones who, like LaVerne Bates, had found masters with whom they could study privately.

LAVERNE
BATES

W e aren't limited by reality nearly as much as we are limited by our own minds—by what we ourselves think we can do," says LaVerne Bates, founder of the first martial arts class for women on the West Coast and perhaps in the entire United States, and one of the first Americans—man or woman—to be instructed by a master in an art of kung fu. "I know the world is limitless to us," she says, "if we will only overcome our own fear."

LaVerne was born LaVerne Hall in 1934 in Oklahoma, the first child and only daughter of a sharecropper family with Cherokee Indian ancestors on both sides. She was expected to be competent and strong, to take care of herself and to work hard.

"My parents wanted a boy for their first born," LaVerne says, "and when I was a child, my father just made me into one. It was the best thing that could've happened, considering the way girls were usually raised. I got a sense of myself as sturdy and strong, which I don't think I would have gotten otherwise. It has been to my advantage all of my life."

LaVerne went hunting and fishing with her father, and she worked alongside him in the fields. Her grandfather, too, treated her "like a boy," and she became his apprentice carpenter.

"When I was ten I helped him build a schoolhouse," she recalls. "It was wonderful."

LaVerne didn't go to school herself until she was eight years old and could walk the three miles to the one-room cabin that served grades one through eight in Okfuskee County.

"My mother walked me half-way," she remembers. "Then she turned back to the farm and I was on my own. I was the only one in my grade, and each year I would get a new set of books to work on. My teacher for all those years was a tobacco-chewing minister who loved to tell ghost stories and read poetry out loud. His favorite was Wordsworth's *Evangeline.* He read it so often during the rainy season that I learned it by heart. I still love it, and now I read it to the kids in my own classes while we're working on postures."

LaVerne didn't see any martial arts as a youngster. The only contact she had with the world beyond Okfuskee came through the radio, which she sometimes listened to at the home of Jim and Rebecca Silas, the Halls' nearest neighbors. There was no television in the countryside then, and the nearest movie theatre was thirty miles away. People relied on one another for entertainment, for company, and for help in times of need. It was Jim Silas who taught LaVerne how to weigh cotton, and it was Rebecca Silas who cared for Mrs. Hall the winter she was sick, stopping by almost every day to help with "the babies"—LaVerne's three younger brothers—and to cook a meal for the family, letting LaVerne help and teaching her "never to waste anything."

The Silases were black, and LaVerne's mother often used them to illustrate her conviction that "the beautiful human soul resides equally in bodies of all shapes, colors, and sizes."

Sometimes LaVerne and her brothers were invited to their cousins' house—there were four cousins, all boys—to listen to "the fights," boxing matches featuring the popular world champion Joe Louis. Afterwards, they would go outside and box.

"I was always expected to take a turn," she says now. "After all, I was one of the boys."

But the freedom she enjoyed came to an end when LaVerne reached twelve.

"Oh, adolescence!" she says. "When I think back on those years and all those problems—it just seems overwhelming. I had been the very model of a tomboy—and suddenly, I wasn't allowed to do anything! Suddenly, I was to brush my hair two times a day and keep it shiny. I wasn't to wear braids but ribbons. My stockings were always to be neat and clean and not muddy from sliding into first base. I was not allowed to play with the boys my own age who were my dearest friends. And I wasn't given an explanation. I must have asked 'why' a thousand times, but my mother never would give me an answer. It was just, 'Come inside—you're too big for that now!' I know she thought she was doing the right thing, but it was terrible."

When she was fourteen, LaVerne felt so closed in by the new rules that she ran away from home. She hadn't gone far before she was picked up by the local sheriff and, at the request of her parents, kept in jail overnight.

"When I saw those gates closing, I was the most frightened I've ever been in my life. I didn't run away again, but I was still confused and hurt by the limits that had been placed on my behavior. I knew they were false and that they had nothing to do with my real nature. But I had no choice and I just went underground."

LaVerne turned more and more to books, reading "everything" from Zane Grey to *Little Women,* but preferring stories of challenge and adventure. In her sophomore year of high school, she became eligible for the girls' softball team and became its most enthusiastic member. Sports and teams for girls were major activities in the rural high schools of the Midwest at that time, and LaVerne's parents had no objection. By the time the season was over, LaVerne had pitched her team to victory in the league and fallen "desperately" in love with the coach, an even-tempered, idealistic young athlete named James "Jay" Barnard.

LaVerne finished high school in three years and went on to nearby Central State College, where Jay Barnard was studying for an advanced degree. She enrolled in the nursing program and just before finishing it, she and Jay were married. When her mother died, late in the spring, she took in her youngest brother, Ronnie.

The next year was 1954, the year the Supreme Court ended segregation in the public schools. Until then, under a policy that claimed to provide "separate but equal" educational facilities, black children and white children throughout the South and in border states like Oklahoma had not been allowed to attend the same schools. Now the Supreme Court stated that that policy was essentially unfair and harmful—and unconstitutional. All public schools were to be integrated, attended by children of both races equally.

The school where Jay taught was desegregated without any problems. Nevertheless, the Supreme Court's decision had tapped

LaVerne demonstrates with student Evelyn Afenir the proper response to an attempted attack: she grabs the assailant's arm and pulls it down, at the same time launching a palm-heel strike of her own.

a hornet's nest of feelings and fears. The atmosphere even in Oklahoma was very tense.

"People sometimes forget how bad things really were," LaVerne says, "how very unequal the separate facilities were, and how much anger and bad feeling there was in the white community when the Court made its decision. The worst and ugliest feelings came tumbling out of even the most unlikely people. I am not a crusader in any way, but I found myself becoming more and more outspoken."

LaVerne was working in a hospital at the time. The emergency room treated patients of all races, and so did the delivery room in the obstetrical ward. But aside from that, black patients were treated and housed on a separate "black floor" staffed by black nurses. Soon after the school desegregation decision, LaVerne asked to be assigned there.

"I wanted to make my position clear and I wanted to be of help," LaVerne says. "In the months that followed I acquired something of a reputation—good or bad depending on your point of view."

LaVerne worked with several of the civil rights groups that began to be active in the South in the 1950s, and her family urged her to take a course in self-defense.

"I already knew how to fight," LaVerne says, "just because of my upbringing, and I wasn't particularly afraid. But there was a lot of violent talk in the air then, and a lot of people had already gotten hurt, and it did seem like a good idea to get some skills down really solid."

LaVerne looked for months, but a self-defense class that would accept her was hard to find. Finally the instructor of a judo class that was oriented toward self-defense said he would allow her to enroll.

"He warned me that he wasn't going to treat me any differently from his other students—which thrilled me to death! Unfortunately, it wasn't true. I was ridiculed and I was used as an example of weakness. I stayed because I'm stubborn and because even though I'd had to 'come inside' when I was twelve, I knew I could keep up with the men if I was allowed to try. I did. I got the skills I needed, and then I left."

LaVerne and Jay were active members of the Methodist Church. During the Christmas vacation of 1956, when parishioners were asked to share their homes with children from a nearby orphanage, they took in a thirteen-year-old Indian boy named James. He and Ronnie quickly became good friends, and LaVerne and Jay felt very drawn to him. When the vacation was over, they made arrangements to have him stay on. Within the year, they adopted him officially.

"Our household was busy and the years were flying by," LaVerne says. "Jay was happy teaching school, he was as active as ever, and there was nothing to give us any warning of what was coming. He had a few headaches, which we didn't pay any attention to at all. And then one evening, he had a coronary and within minutes, he was dead."

The year was 1960. Ronnie and James were almost grown. LaVerne, a widow at twenty-six, felt very much alone. She continued to work in the hospital, but she was drawn more and more into the struggle for civil rights, which was gaining momentum throughout the South. Marches, demonstrations, voter registration drives, and "freedom rides" brought people who were committed to racial justice into the most remote areas of the South. Early in 1961, LaVerne herself joined a crew of "moderators" who traveled throughout Oklahoma and the neighboring states, working for the desegregation of everything from roller-skating rinks, picnic grounds, and libraries, to hotels, ball parks, and public pools and beaches. While she was on the road LaVerne met Fenia Woo, a Chinese woman who was also working for civil rights. She was compassionate, dedicated, reserved—and a master of two arts of kung fu, the soft flowing art of t'ai chi ch'uan, and a hard style from northern China called *sil lum.*

"We traveled together and often roomed together," LaVerne recalls, "and I used to watch her doing her t'ai chi exercises. After a while she invited me to become her student. We hardly ever spoke. She wasn't someone you could just chat with. I once asked her why a form was done in a particular way and she looked at me for a full minute before answering. 'You'll know when the time is right,' she said. 'Make it part of you and then you'll understand.' "

It wasn't an answer, but coming from Fenia, LaVerne found it acceptable. She studied t'ai chi, and then *sil lum p'ai,* the harder kung fu style Fenia also practiced. After a while she concentrated on *sil lum p'ai* exclusively. LaVerne didn't know it at the time, but Fenia was breaking an ancient tradition by teaching kung fu to someone who was not of Chinese descent. Though Fenia would not discuss her own background, LaVerne learned that she came from a large family with a long history in kung fu practice, and that she had received her own training at home.

"Fenia Woo's incredible skill as an artist and her sensitivity as a human being went beyond anything I had ever experienced," LaVerne says. "She was there for me in a way I can't really describe. She became the most special friend I've ever had."

LaVerne was already physically strong when she began her training, but more important to her progress was the "driving force" within her.

"In all the martial arts," she says, "you are pushed beyond your limits. And it's hard. It's hard for everyone. But there is a force within us which makes us want to work hard and the martial arts bring that force into focus. I think I had access to it from the beginning, and that was my gift and my strong point when I began to work with Fenia."

LaVerne, 5'4" and 130 pounds, was not especially agile or limber.

"I had to practice and work with my body a lot. Most of us do, though when you see someone who is limber you just assume they've always been that way. When I began, I could hardly kick above groin level. As a result, I concentrated on getting height into my kicks and now I have more kicking in my art than anything else. I know it's been said before, but I'll say it again—nothing that's important comes easy."

After over a year of working and traveling together, LaVerne and Fenia decided to make a trip to the Far East.

"I don't even remember which one of us decided first," LaVerne says. "But suddenly we were making plans. For her, it was a trip she been thinking about for years. For me, it was the adventure I had always wanted, and it was a chance to get closer to the martial arts, which were becoming such an important part of my life."

LaVerne and Fenia traveled through the Far East the way they had traveled through the southern states—together, but totally independent, speaking very little, sharing a basic itinerary but self-contained on a day-to-day basis.

"In Hong Kong, she took me to visit a kung fu studio," LaVerne remembers, "and because of her I was allowed to observe. But most of the time, we went our separate ways. She might go off to visit a friend and I would go off to walk through the city. I wouldn't see her again until nine or ten at night when I'd return to the hotel to find her, as often as not, meditating or doing her forms. She was at least twenty years older than I was, but her energy was endless."

Back in the United States, Fenia settled in California and LaVerne returned to the Midwest and a job on the children's ward of a private hospital. Several of the children suffered from asthma and LaVerne asked for permission to teach them kung fu breathing exercises.

"I had had asthma myself as a child," she says. "It wasn't nearly as serious as it was for the children I was working with, but it helped me understand how frightening it was for them. I thought the kung fu breathing exercises would help to strengthen the diaphragm, and so help them gain control of their breathing. And it did! It was a wonderful class, the children benefitted tremendously, and it made me love kung fu all the more."

LaVerne had no one to train with, so she practiced on her own, working out daily in her home and sometimes in the yard outside.

"Kung fu had become an art for me," she says. "And I wanted to be an artist. I would have trained no matter where I was or how hard it was, or what anyone said or thought. Every time I got to a new level of understanding I'd wonder why I hadn't seen it before, why I hadn't understood it before, and I couldn't wait to reach the

LaVerne teaches her students to tuck their heads down to escape from a choke and to thrust the arm down to prevent an arm lock.

next level. I missed Fenia very much, but I knew I could be my own teacher if I had to."

A year later, in the spring of 1963, LaVerne was on her way to California too, newly married to Gilbert Bates, a student of the martial arts who loved them as much as she did. "We moved to California for all the usual reasons," she says with a smile, "and for some special ones of our own—mainly the fact that the best teachers of the Chinese martial arts were living there. For me, that meant Fenia. But Gil, who had studied a Korean art and was fascinated by kung fu, was looking for a teacher too, and California was the place to find one."

LaVerne accepted a job in a private medical office and Gil found a job as a teacher. It wasn't long before he was enrolled in the studio of Grandmaster Ark Yuey Wong, one of the first, some say the very first, Chinese kung fu master in the United States to open his school to students who were not of Chinese descent. Before that, kung fu training had been simply unavailable unless, like LaVerne, you were fortunate enough to meet someone who would instruct you in private. LaVerne, already an advanced student, trained with Grandmaster Wong from time to time and was recognized by him as an artist of accomplishment. But her own main teacher and inspiration was Fenia, whom she now saw and worked with daily.

"My art began to grow in a new way," LaVerne recalls. "I began to work with weapons, and I found that they were my greatest challenge and my greatest joy. It was Fenia who was my model. She was five feet tall, and 104 pounds, but she was strong and she handled weapons with grace and power you had to see to believe. She taught me the staff, the double sword, the dagger, the double dagger and the tiger fork—like a pitchfork only much larger. I liked them all, and I think it was because deep down in my mind I felt that of all the things in the martial arts women aren't supposed to be able to do, weapons are the most extreme. When I worked with them I felt more strongly than ever that women can do anything."

LaVerne works with and teaches the quon do, *a Chinese weapon that may date from the first century* B.C.E.

LaVerne's favorite weapon was the *quan do,* five pounds in weight, and 6'4" in length. "I think it's the hardest weapon to develop any skill with," she says, "because it's so big and cumbersome. And that's why I loved it and why I still love it. Conquering that weapon was like conquering all the false ideas we have about women's weakness and helplessness. Society does not help us become strong. We have to do it ourselves."

In 1967, Gilbert opened the Bates Kung Fu Studio. LaVerne continued to work as a nurse during the day, but she taught classes at the studio at night. The Bates Kung Fu Studio would have welcomed women, but none came to enroll. "Not one woman even called on the phone," LaVerne recalls, "not even to inquire!"

Realizing that women were not going to find their way to her, LaVerne determined to find them. And if "mixed" (male and female) classes felt to most women like men's classes with a few women thrown in, she would offer a class for women only. She contacted local schools and the county Department of Parks and Recreation. She demonstrated, spoke, and introduced herself at street fairs, community picnics, festivals, and other events that gave women a chance to see her and talk to her about the martial arts and what they had to offer. In the spring of 1968, after months of work, an official "women's class" began at the Bates Kung Fu Studio. It was the first women's martial arts class on the West Coast and, by most accounts, in the entire country.

Grandmaster Wong endorsed LaVerne's efforts, and Fenia came daily, without being asked, to work out with her, to help structure the class, and to advise the students. "She was always there when someone needed her," LaVerne says.

Sometimes Fenia brought with her other Chinese artists who were interested in helping LaVerne and the women's class. Two of them, Nathaniel Ho and Meeyalin Chiang, became LaVerne's close associates and after Fenia, her most important teachers. The class itself flourished.

"I saw women and girls blossom as they overcame the false limitations their upbringing had placed upon them. They dropped the subdued manner women so often assume around men. They were able to work to the utmost of their ability and it was astonishing how fast some of them learned. To this day, my greatest joy as a teacher is in seeing a woman come in feeling timid and alone and watching her grow into a strong, self-confident person."

As La Verne's students began to develop competence in kung fu, she accompanied them to tournaments and prepared them for competition. But what she found at some events was terrible.

"We must improve the conditions under which women compete," she wrote in 1976 in an article for *Black Belt Magazine,* the best-selling martial arts magazine in America. LaVerne listed her grievances at length—from judges whose attention wandered when women were performing and divisions that placed adult women together with children, to prizes and trophies given out as personal favors because women's events just were not taken seriously.

"I refused to participate in tournaments that were insulting to women," LaVerne says. "People tell me I've had some influence."

LaVerne's class also became something of a counseling and referral service for women who were survivors of rape and battering. "To this day, not a month goes by without a woman calling and asking for help because her husband or boyfriend has beaten her and she doesn't know what to do. I didn't know how common the situation was when I began my class, but I soon found out."

Within a few years, LaVerne's class had grown so large and become the hub of so many activities that she decided to separate her students from Gilbert's school and open an independent women's studio.

"I wanted something more for my students than a place to train," she says. "I wanted a place where a woman could come and share herself and receive what she needed in return."

Today LaVerne's students participate with her in the management and running of the LaVerne Bates Women's Kung Fu Studio. Over the years, the school has offered a wide variety of classes, from kung fu training for children as young as four, to workshops for battered women, seminars in career guidance, classes in nutrition and self-improvement, and most recently, meditation.

"The things we offer depend on what we think we need," LaVerne says. "They will surely change over the years. But my goal will remain the same. I want women to overcome fear and false limits. I want to use the martial arts to help women become strong, free-thinking individuals who will be inspired to attempt their dreams."

T'ai Chi Ch'uan

T'AI CHI CH'UAN IS THE CHINESE KUNG FU ART THAT STRESSES SMOOTH, FLUID movements, slow, deep breathing, and relaxation. It is often practiced for the sake of general health and well-being, but it is a very effective fighting system too. Symbolized by the half-dark, half-light circle which stands for the universe, and based on the ancient saying that "meditation in motion is a thousand times better than meditation in repose," t'ai chi ch'uan has been loved for centuries as an art that offers strength, health, long life, and a tranquil spirit.

At the heart of t'ai chi ch'uan training is the solo exercise, a series of postures—some with lovely and suggestive names like "Embrace Tiger and Return to Mountain" and "Step Forward to the Seven Stars"—arranged in a specific sequence. As they move from one posture to another, t'ai chi artists look as if they were moving under water or performing a formal dance in slow motion. They must be totally relaxed as they move, with no tightness or tension anywhere, so that their inner energy, their *ch'i*, thought to be much more important than muscular strength, can flow freely.

Although the solo exercise is often done for its own sake, each posture has a fighting function, which can easily be seen if the exercise is done quickly. In fact, students are supposed to imagine an opponent as they move. At more advanced levels, students work against real opponents. Using the movements learned in the solo exercise, and the principles of relaxation and *ch'i* development, they learn a skill called the *interpretation of strength*. It is the heart of t'ai chi fighting: the ability to sense the flow of energy in an opponent, to anticipate the move she is about to make and foil it before it can be completed. T'ai chi is a defensive system, but when attacked, a t'ai chi artist is a fighter of legendary skill.

"If your opponent does not move," says the *T'ai Chi Ch'uan Classics*, a work which may go back to the seventeenth century, "you do not move. But at his slightest stir, you have already anticipated it and are enabled to move first."

You do not meet force with force. Instead, you quickly yield, providing no resistance, so that the force loses its power. When your opponent comes at you, the *Classics* says, "he feels as if there is no end to the emptiness he encounters." Given his momentum, a slight push or pull will topple him.

Historians are not certain about the origins of t'ai chi. According to some accounts, it was created in the fourteenth century by a monk named Chang San-feng, who thought the older systems had drifted too far from Taoism and had become too hard. Whether or not this is the case, t'ai chi does embody the ideas of Lao Tsu in ways the other "harder" arts do not. Lao Tsu believed that softness and suppleness, balance and harmony were essential to the good life, and that true strength lay in yielding. "Nothing under heaven is softer or more yielding than water," he wrote in *The Way and the Power*. "But when it attacks things hard and resistant there is not one of them that can prevail . . . in all cases, the yielding conquers the resistant and the soft conquers the hard."

Lao Tsu thought that the ultimate principles of the universe could be understood, and peace and tranquility achieved, if we followed the proper path or "way" (tao). T'ai chi ch'uan, which means "supreme ultimate (t'ai chi) fist (ch'uan)" was intended to be such a way.

PATTIE
DACANAY

Pattie Dacanay moves slowly, with a calm presence that seems to come from somewhere deep inside. Her dark eyes are clear, her face serene, and when she speaks, you know you are listening to a woman who is at ease in the world and at peace with herself. You can't imagine that she was ever different. But she was.

"If you had met me ten years ago," Pattie says with a smile, "you certainly would not have said I was serene. A more likely word would have been 'frantic.' "

Ten years ago, Pattie had never heard of t'ai chi ch'uan, the ancient Chinese art of which she is now a master. She was living in Seattle, Washington, working in the sales department of a company that handled tapes and records, and she was married to a rock and roll musician.

"I was a rock and roll musician's wife, and everything you hear about that is true. My husband's band was the number one band in the city, so they were constantly working. And I was at all the gigs, every weekend, handling public relations, taking care of everyone. My head was filled with noise, and I was always exhausted because during the week when they slept late and kept their own hours, I was at my 'other' job."

At a friend's urging, Pattie visited a small studio in Seattle's

Chinatown where t'ai chi ch'uan was being taught.

"I was entranced," Pattie says, "from the moment I stepped into the room."

The studio was silent and immaculate, as austere as a "monastery cell." Photographs of t'ai chi masters hung on one wall. Classical Chinese weapons were mounted on another. And beside the open window was an altar holding oranges, incense, and autumn leaves. The students moved very slowly, without making a sound.

"It was like poetry. It was like a ballet. The range of motion and the balance they maintained in slow motion were incredible to me. I had never seen anything like it before, or anything like that atmosphere, the silent peaceful energy that just filled the room. I

Pattie demonstrates the single whip, a hand position in the Wu *style t'ai chi form. The fingertips touch in a lotus blossom pattern, and the ends of all fingers must be flush. Pattie practices by tapping her fingertips on a table or into the palm of her left hand. If one finger is out of line, she can feel it immediately.*

didn't understand what it was, but I knew it was what I needed, and I felt as though I belonged there."

Master John S. S. Leong, the founder and chief instructor of the school, was a quiet man with "an aura of strength and dignity." He had been trained in China, in the traditional, highly disciplined way.

"There was no outside world competing for his attention," Pattie says. "You could see his concentration, his full commitment in every move he made. T'ai chi was the center of life for him. His identification with it was complete, and he expected his students to feel the same way."

Most of the students seemed to be in awe of Master Leong. They could hardly speak to him. But Pattie felt a special bond with him from the beginning, and she quickly became his most devoted student.

"I had no special gift," she says, "except my stubbornness. My family always said that the harder you work, the more you get back, and I believed that. If I hadn't, I would have given up. I've seen hundreds of people come and go over the years, but I was just determined."

Pattie doesn't advise other people to go about it the way she did. "I pushed myself to the limit," she says. "I was told the flexibility and balance would come in time, but I couldn't wait. I forced myself to hold stretches I wasn't ready for, and I was in pain, I was in agony for months. I could barely walk up and down the stairs, but I was willing to go through anything in order to do the postures perfectly. Now I am extremely limber and I have experienced some of the ecstasy of my art—and I hope I'll have it for many years to come, because I'll never forget the agony."

There are no ranks in t'ai chi. You learn certain forms and then you go on to the next ones. Pattie's growing mastery was acknowledged by her *Sifu* (Chinese for "respected teacher") when, after

Pattie practices the gee fi gim, *a single-edged sword form from the hard* hung gar *style of kung fu. A form from a hard style is often taught to t'ai chi students to help them develop speed, agility, and timing.*

one year's training, he invited her to learn an advanced form done with a sword.

"I resisted working with a sword for a while because it seemed so foreign and external," she says. "But my Sifu taught me to think of it as an extension of my body. He said that working with it would strengthen my concentration and my balance. And it did, and I loved it."

Sifu Leong also asked Pattie to teach beginning students in one of his branch schools. She had mixed feelings. "I felt as though I was being kicked out of the nest, and I didn't want to go."

Pattie turned out to be an excellent teacher, and in fact, while growing up, had planned to be one. The oldest child in a family of four children, she had always taken care of her younger brothers and sisters, and she had been something of a "mother hen" to an extended family that included thirty cousins.

"My family was very close and very big," she laughs. "We were everywhere, even though neither of my parents was originally from Seattle. My father was born in the Philippines and my mother was born in South Dakota. But soon after they settled in Seattle, the whole family gravitated there. I was usually put in charge of the kids, and I always thought I would be a teacher."

Pattie had been set to attend the University of Washington and to major in education there before being sidetracked by her job, her marriage, and her husband's career. Now that she was teaching t'ai chi, she felt as though she had come full circle. And the more she taught and studied, the clearer it became that she had found the center of her life in "the t'ai chi spirit."

"The things I had pushed for so hard in the beginning began to come naturally, and I really began to change, especially my breathing, which is so essential in t'ai chi. Each movement is done to an exhale or an inhale, and you work and work to increase the depth of your breathing. It was after about a year that I could feel my breath sink, and I began to breathe abdominally, the way you are supposed to. I could take in more air, I breathed more slowly, and my movements slowed down too. That's when the real fluidity and the real fine tuning of your body begins."

She began to study Chinese herbal medicine, massage, callig-

raphy, and nutrition. She took on responsibility for classes in Sifu
Leong's outlying schools, and was soon the head t'ai chi trainer at
the University of Washington branch and the branch in suburban
Burien. Many times, after her classes were over, she would return
to central Seattle to work out on her own until after midnight.
Inevitably, as her priorities changed, the other parts of her life
changed too. The differences showed up first in her marriage.

"I had always been my husband's main support. I was with him
and for him seven days a week, and even in my own mind, what he
was doing took first place. Suddenly I wasn't there anymore. He
felt neglected—and he was right. I *was* neglecting him, compared
with the way I had been before. But I couldn't go back. Something
had begun to grow in me and it was important, and I wanted to
devote myself to it entirely."

Pattie and her husband parted without rancor. "We didn't have
the kinds of personal problems you hear about. But I had to let go of
him and be on my own."

The second shift had to do with her job. Pattie had been aware
for some time that she was not being treated fairly. She was doing
the same work that the men in her company were doing, but she
did not have the same title, and she did not get the same salary.
Now she spoke up, and when her employer refused to upgrade
her, she quit.

In 1978, Pattie made the last shift. She decided to leave Seattle
altogether and move to Athens, Ohio. A good friend had decided
to go to school there, and Pattie felt it was time she too set out on
her own. This move seemed to be what all the other changes had
been leading to. Nevertheless, it was difficult.

"I was leaving the city in which I had been born and raised,
leaving my friends, my family, my school. But hardest of all was
leaving my teacher, Master Leong," Pattie says. "I thank him every
day for what he shared with me."

Athens is a small college town in a part of southeast Ohio that

With two of her students at Special Training 1982, Pattie practices the "brush knee and twist" step. She enjoys the feeling of "bonded energy" she gets working with others, even though each movement flows with the individual's own breath.

has been honored in Indian legend and history as one of the earth's great gathering places for spiritual energy. Pattie loved the area and had no trouble getting settled there. She proved to be an excellent organizer.

"When I arrived," she says, "I could count on the fingers of one hand how many people knew what t'ai chi was. There certainly was not a ready audience for it. But an audience developed."

Pattie began by holding t'ai chi demonstrations to which she invited people from the press, the university, the media, and the general public. She visited schools, social service centers, hospitals. Newspaper articles were written about her and about t'ai chi. A radio station asked her to do a short weekly broadcast about t'ai chi and other aspects of Chinese culture. The University of Ohio invited her to make a series of programs for its cable television project. In the course of the twelve segments, Pattie explained some of the basic exercises that she thinks are the most important part of early training.

"The exercises were simple—from just bending over and touching your toes to standing on one leg and raising the other out to the side to about knee height, holding it, and returning it to the ground. But I would explain that if they did the exercises correctly, with breathing and relaxation, every muscle in the body would have been well stretched, and if they did them daily, they would increase their range of motion and their flexibility almost without limit. I usually did the exercises the way I thought most of the people in the audience would do them, but sometimes I did them to my own capacity to show them what could be achieved. Flexibility and balance come to everyone with enough repetitions. Even with older people who have lost it, it can be regained."

When the television project was finished, Pattie was invited to teach in person at the university's Continuing Education Center. By the spring, she was holding workshops for health educators, professional dancers, and the Athens Senior Citizen's Center. Soon she established her own school.

The next winter, Pattie made a trip to the island of Taiwan, where the most accomplished t'ai chi artists in the world can be found. As in China itself, almost everyone in Taiwan practices one martial art or another. They practice early in the morning, in the fields and squares of every town and village.

"I think of myself as a pretty energetic person," Pattie says, "but in Taiwan, I felt lazy! People of all ages were outside and working out at 4:00 A.M.! On the first morning, they were finished by the time I got there! Training is their first commitment, their top priority, seven days a week, rain or shine."

Pattie was primarily interested in the self-defense and fighting aspects of t'ai chi, since that was the area in which she had the least experience. She watched each of the masters at work in Taipei Park, and then decided to study with Sifu Tsheng, the leading practitioner of *tui-sau*, "push-hands," the t'ai chi technique that comes closest to sparring.

Push-hands starts out with two people facing each other, feet planted in one spot, wrists and arms up and touching lightly. As one person slowly pushes the arms and wrists of the other in slow circular motions, the other yields, then pushes back. Feet do not move, and as you yield and push in turn, great care must be taken to maintain your balance.

"One pushes, one retreats, flowing as one, always connected," Pattie explains. "In Chinese they say that you 'eat the other's mind.' You feel the other person's movement from its inception. You yield to it, bend with it, so it loses its force and does not push you over."

On advanced levels, push-hands can be very fast and aggressive. On the highest level, you may work "free style," moving about the floor, maintaining contact with your partner and keeping your balance while trying to get your partner to lose hers. Expertise comes only with experience.

"As you learn to relax your own muscles," Pattie says, "you can feel the other person's tension and energy. It is transmitted through the hands, arms, shoulders, like an electric shock, mild but constant, and you know when your opponent is going to move, unless she too can relax her muscles. A trained person can fool you, and feel the second your balance is not rooted—and then over you go! The sensitivity involved takes years to develop. My teacher used to say, 'A thousand repetitions is a good beginning.' Anyone can push. Few can feel."

Pattie was introduced to Sifu Tsheng as a t'ai chi teacher from America. He had never instructed an American woman before, and he welcomed her courteously. The next day, she arrived in the park in time to do the stretching exercises she still considers the most important part of daily training. The noises from the bus terminal just outside the main gate didn't affect her concentration

Pattie practices the tai gek gim, *a t'ai chi sword form that uses a double-edged sword. Following this low stance, Pattie must rise on one leg and fully extend the other, while slicing outward with the sword in her left hand and blocking overhead with her right hand. The gracefulness of this form intrigued her from the beginning, though she found it as difficult to learn as it is to describe.*

at all, and as she soon realized, she was more flexible than anyone there.

"I stretched my foot up to the branch above my head and held it there for several minutes to get a good stretch—and several other students came around to watch. They watched me do the other exercises for balance and flexibility my Sifu had taught me. The next day, a few students came to ask me whether I would be their teacher. I was so honored I hardly knew how to respond. But I had to tell them that I was there to study and learn myself and I just couldn't teach."

Sifu Tsheng thought Pattie's concentration, agility, and timing were extraordinary. Before she had been there a week, he invited her to be his own partner in the push-hands exercise.

"I was deeply grateful to my Sifu for the training he gave me, because everyone recognized it right away. I was treated like a queen. It was incredible."

Pattie's legs and back were already strong, but still she was not prepared for the intensity of the work she did with Sifu Tsheng.

"We started out with basic slow motion exercises, and at first I could only work with him for half an hour at a time. He pushed me so hard I was arched into a back bend. I hurt so bad I could hardly get out of bed in the morning. But after a while I could work for three hours with just a break to shake out a little every hour or so."

When masters from other parts of the island came to Taipei Park to pay their respects to Sifu Tsheng, he introduced them to Pattie and invited them to work with her. "Their strength and experience in the martial arts were to their advantage. My flexibility and sensitivity to movement—all of which I had learned, none of which was natural to me—was to my advantage. I didn't get surprised very often."

Sifu Tsheng invited Pattie to take part in the push-hands competition at the upcoming festival of the World T'ai Chi Association. Although she had only been training for two months, he assured her that she would win in her class. But Pattie could not stay for the festival. Her visa would be up before then, and she would have to return to the United States. Nevertheless, since only masters are allowed to enter, the invitation was a great honor. Pattie left Taiwan feeling encouraged, inspired, and immensely strengthened. But her good feelings disappeared when she returned to Ohio.

"I guess it was a kind of cultural shock," she says. "And maybe I should have expected it. But I didn't. I had felt so much at home in Taiwan, and I had been welcomed so warmly and so completely by the people. In Ohio, I felt as though I was standing alone again,

Four sequential movements from the t'ai chi form. Continuous motion and flow follow the individual's breathing. Maintaining fluidity and balance is only learned with many repetitions.

after having been part of a real community. I felt cut off and isolated in a way I never had before."

But as the weeks turned to months, Pattie found new ways to use her t'ai chi energy. When one of her students became pregnant, Pattie realized how helpful t'ai chi exercises would be for women during pregnancy and childbirth. She began working with her student and then agreed to be with her when the time came for the baby to be born.

"It was the first birth I ever attended," Pattie says. "The little boy, Miles, is my godson and I feel now that there is a wonderful bond between us."

Shortly after Miles's birth, Pattie began to work as an apprentice to two local midwives and thought she would like to become a midwife herself. But then she had to miss a t'ai chi class because she was at a birth. It was the only class she had ever missed.

"I realized that I couldn't commit myself to an apprenticeship at that time," she says. "It required a person who could attend meetings regularly—be able to run at a moment's notice at the time of labor—and I just couldn't do that. My own t'ai chi training would not have had such an overwhelming effect on my entire life if my Sifu was not at class when he said he would be. He instilled discipline in me because of his dedication. I wanted to do the same for my students."

Later in the year, Pattie began to work with patients at the Athens Mental Health Center. She designed a program of modified t'ai chi exercises as a relaxation-movement class. She volunteered her services and asked the center only for space and permission.

"The director of activities, whom I had met on our local women's volleyball team, said I wouldn't have any trouble getting permission, but she warned me not to be disappointed if no one came to my classes," Pattie remembers, "or if no one came back a second time. But the classes have been an unqualified, 100 percent success."

One class is made up of women who are considered so disturbed they are kept in a locked ward.

"When they first came, they were very skeptical and suspicious," Pattie says. "I would ask them to relax and close their eyes and I would see them peeking at me when they thought I wasn't looking. But slowly, we managed to relax together and then we began to move together. By the time class is over, they are always calmer and stronger."

Pattie also works with aged men and women from the geriatric ward. Some of them have been on medication for years. They suffer from twitches and other involuntary movements, and their coordination is very poor. "Movement of almost any kind is difficult for them. But they work hard, and they improve. In some cases, I can actually see them getting better."

Pattie would gladly continue her work with these people on a volunteer basis. But the center is now committed to the program and has put her on salary. She has also been invited to increase the number and size of her classes.

In addition to running her own school and the work she does at the health center, Pattie also works at an out-patient clinic with people who suffer from arthritis, with a professional dance troupe, and with a university theater group, which contacted her when they were performing a play involving a Vietnamese wedding cermony where tranquility was the hallmark. After the play's run, she was offered a permanent job with the drama department at the University of Ohio.

"The more I train, the more energy I have," Pattie says. "It seems endless. Master Leong told me years ago that this would happen, but it still feels like a surprise!"

Pattie worked with a group of holistic health educators to organize her most ambitious project so far: an annual retreat to the countryside. This year, close to one hundred people will attend. The retreat, which is held at a farm, is especially important to Pattie because it is a celebration of the cycles of the earth and the balance of nature. As such, it is closely tied to the Taoist idea of the harmony of the universe.

"We need to find ways of relating to nature that are not possessive and destructive," she says. "We need traditions and rituals that celebrate the harmony and beauty of the universe, and the solstice is one of them. If we can experience the harmony of the universe, we will be able to find it in our own lives, too."

The retreat emphasizes the connection between respect for the planet and loving care of the self. It features workshops in various aspects of natural and holistic health care, methods of self-healing, group meditation, and of course t'ai chi exercises. Although it didn't start out that way, the event is now for women only.

"Men were in on the early planning stage," Pattie says, "but after a while, the core group became an all-women's group. I think now that it's very important for women to work together. The bonding that takes place when we do is just incredible. Women have had so little power in the past, but now that we are coming together and finding our voices, I think we will be a great force for balance and joy in the universe. I have more and more respect for our capabilities as time goes by."

Today Pattie lives in a one-room cabin in the woods thirteen miles outside of Athens. The cabin has no running water and no electricity. It is heated only by a wood stove. She is happy there and with the work she is doing in Athens. But she doesn't think she will stay forever. "I feel that there were important reasons for me to be in Athens. But I don't think I'm going to be here for the rest of my life."

Where will she go? She doesn't know.

"One thing will lead to the next," she says, "and things will work out the way they are supposed to. Ten years ago, I could not have predicted the direction my life would take. But I am very happy with the way things have gone, and I have absolutely no regrets. I just try to do the right thing in the present, and I try to be open to the meaning of the present, and to the things it makes possible."

"The world is ruled by letting things take their course," said Lao Tsu. That is the principle Pattie lives by.

Tae Kwon Do

TAE KWON DO IS THE KOREAN ART OF EMPTY-HANDED FIGHTING. *TAE* means "to kick or smash with one's feet." *Kwon* means "to destroy with one's hand or fist." *Do* means "the way." Like karate, its Okinawan-Japanese counterpart, tae kwon do is a strong, fast system, primarily but not entirely defensive. Practitioners punch, kick, jump, block, and dodge, and although tae kwon do is most admired for its spectacular leg work, many kinds of hand strikes are also taught, including some designed to be done while on horseback.

Tae kwon do is weaponless, but it teaches methods of dealing with armed opponents. Some styles teach methods of throwing an opponent, and many include the circular hand movements that are typical of Chinese systems. Breathing exercises, also based on ancient Chinese ideas about bodily strength and energy, are considered essential ways of generating power. Special importance is placed on the breathing you do as you meet an attack, for which the method of *"jiptjung,"* which means "power gathering," is central.

Like the other Korean martial systems, tae kwon do has its origins in the fighting arts of seventh-century China. They were brought to Korea primarily through the efforts of the monarch of the southeast kingdom of Silla, Queen Songdok, who sent war-

100

riors to China to study them and established a school near her court where her subjects could learn them. This school produced warriors of legendary daring and skill. A code of ethics known as *hwarang-do,* "the Way of the Flower of Manhood," also developed there. *Hwarang-do* taught that the virtues of character—loyalty, honesty, courage, and justice—were the warrior's virtues, and that the warrior's spirit must be as honorable as his body was strong.

When it first came to Korea, empty-handed fighting was called *t'ang-su* ("T'ang hand") in honor of the T'ang dynasty, which ruled China at the time the arts developed. But by the tenth century, when distinctively Korean techniques and styles had emerged, empty-handed fighting came to be called by the Korean name, *kwonpup.* According to a military document of the fifteenth century, *kwonpup* included over one hundred distinct techniques divided into three categories: those that could be used to stun an opponent; those that could be used to make an opponent unconscious; those that could be used to kill.

In modern times, as Korea came more and more under the influence of Japan, the Korean arts were practiced less and less. In the nineteenth century, jujutsu and other Japanese combat arts became very popular in Korea, and *kwonpup*—now called *tae kwonpup* or sometimes just *tae kwon*—was practiced by very few. In the early years of the twentieth century, when Japan took control of Korea outright, Japanese educational programs were introduced into Korean schools, and Korean children were routinely taught the Japanese martial arts. It wasn't until 1945, when Korea became an independent nation, that its own martial tradition and its own martial arts came forward. *Tae kwon* was renamed *tae kwon do* and considered a national art to be returned to a place of honor in Korean life. Since that time, tae kwon do has spread around the world. In 1973, the Korean government established the World Tae Kwon Do Federation. Sunny Graff is one of its finest world champions.

SUNNY
GRAFF

S ometimes the combination of the martial arts and the wom-
en's movement makes me feel there's nothing in the world I
can't do," says Sunny Graff, winner of six gold medals, four
national championships, and the world championship of the
World Tae Kwon Do Federation. Sunny is a defense attorney with
the Franklin County Public Defender's Office of Columbus, Ohio,
founder of Ohio's leading rape-prevention program, and the
founder and instructor of her own tae kwon do club for women.
She thinks she is more effective in everything she does because she
is a martial artist. She doesn't think she would be a martial artist if
she hadn't been a feminist first.

"In 1974, when I began," Sunny says, "the world of the martial
arts was overwhelmingly male. It was next to impossible for a
woman to find her way there, much less to stay. I would not have
stayed myself if I hadn't already been a strong feminist. I remember
looking around the room filled with men—it was like a private
men's club—and I said to myself, 'Well, I'll be!' It was a challenge
and I just couldn't turn it down."

Sunny was raised in Parma Heights, Ohio, a quiet suburb of
Cleveland. With a comfortable home, warm friends, good schools
and a family that was very close, her childhood didn't contain any
hint of the choices she would later make. When she got to high

school, she wanted most of all to be a cheerleader—and she was a good one, who could do splits three ways, left leg front, right leg front, and both legs to the sides. But by the time she was ready to graduate, the rebel in her had begun to surface.

"The anti-war movement and the student culture of the sixties had begun to make themselves felt even in Parma Heights," she says. "There were concerts, protest meetings, poetry readings, drugs, demonstrations—the works. My best friend had a car and we began to go everywhere. I was the first person in my high school to wear the peace symbol—nobody knew what it was."

In 1969, as a freshman at Ohio State University, Sunny gravitated toward the students who seemed the most daring and unconventional. Most of them were men, and it was a point of honor for her to keep up with them and often to be out in front. "There was no dare I wouldn't take," she says. "If they drove fast, I drove faster."

Sunny hitchhiked around the countryside, experimented with drugs, joined anti-Vietnam war rallies and teach-ins, and in the spring, when a massive student anti-war protest was met with a massive police dragnet, spent several days in jail. But although she was active and outspoken, it wasn't until she found the women's movement that she really came into her own.

"It was in the fall of my sophomore year," Sunny remembers, "and things had become very confusing. Politics had gotten more serious and more complicated for me. The drug scene had become a clear disaster. One of my best friends had died over the summer from an overdose and another had committed suicide. Everything seemed to be coming apart."

The first meeting of the Columbus/Ohio State University women's liberation group had been held the year before, but Sunny hadn't been interested then. Now, when the second meeting was announced, she decided to go. The goal of the meeting was to set up working groups and give the women a chance to talk about the issues of concern to them.

This direct kick to the face is a hook kick. It is often used in combination with a roundhouse kick. The hook kick takes down the lead blocking hand, creating an opening for the roundhouse kick that follows.

"It was the most exciting thing I'd ever been to in my life," Sunny says now. "They were talking about things I had never been able to deal with, but always felt on a gut level—that women weren't getting a fair shake, that they were not really respected or valued in our society. My reaction had been to stay away from other women and try to be one of the guys. Now I realized that for all my rebelliousness, I had just accepted the common view of women, the view which said that women weren't worth much. These women were saying that it was all right to be a woman, that we weren't inferior versions of men. They were saying that we could overcome our conditioning and take control of our lives. It was incredible. I remember thinking that with all these women working for change, why, the whole world would be different in ten years!"

Sunny's view of time has changed since then, and she now uses what she calls the Susan B. Anthony time line. "I am fully prepared to spend my life working for changes that won't happen during my lifetime. I prefer my original ten-year plan, but this one is much more realistic."

Before the night was over, Sunny had joined with a group of other women to form the Women's Action Collective—an umbrella group designed to help people start working on specific problems. A psychology major, Sunny also volunteered to work with women's discussion groups and to be a counselor for women in crisis situations. Later, she was an editor of the new *Columbus Free Press*. It was the press which, in the spring, sponsored a "speakout" on rape. Sunny helped to set it up.

"We didn't know how many women would come or exactly how things would go. But speakouts had been held in other places and we were beginning to realize that rape wasn't an individual problem. It was a collective problem affecting all women, and the first step in dealing with it was to get the subject out into the open."

The speakout drew over seventy women, making it one of the most heavily attended events on the calendar. Afterwards, Sunny and other women from the Women's Action Collective formed a permanent group to deal with the issues and help solve the problems they had begun to explore. They called themselves Women Against Rape: WAR.

"We campaigned for better street lights, neighborhood patrols, things like that," Sunny says. "But mostly, we did crisis work. We tried to give direct and immediate aid to women who were survivors of rape. We talked to them, stayed with them, helped them to a hospital or a doctor, went with them to court, and generally did whatever needed to be done."

By the spring of 1973, Sunny's last term in college, she was working not only with WAR but also with the Rape Reduction Unit, a civic group made up of police officers and staff members from local mental hospitals. She was president of the Columbus/ Ohio State women's liberation group, was editor, writer, and graphic designer of the *Free Press* community newspaper (circulation 30,000), and at Bowling Green University, Dennison University, and her own Ohio State, she gave public talks on the subject of violence against women. In March, she co-founded Fan the Flames!, a bookstore devoted to women's issues and women's studies. In April, she appeared on the "Phil Donahue Show" to speak about "Organizing in the Women's Movement." In June, when she graduated, her grades were mediocre, but she had learned a great deal.

Sunny found a job with the Columbus court system as a bond investigator, but the work she was doing for the women's movement, especially for WAR, was still the most important to her. She was working to establish a new Rape Crisis Center, which would enlarge and stabilize the services offered by WAR, when a good friend and feminist, Toni Goman, was murdered.

"I had been doing crisis work for a long time," Sunny says, "and had seen a great deal of violence. But when Toni was killed, it was more than I could take in. It was a savage murder, and there was nothing 'personal' about it. She wasn't killed because she was Toni Goman. Any other women would have done. I was overwhelmed by the reality of violence against women and I couldn't function. It was the worst period of my life."

A few months later, a friend introduced Sunny to the martial arts. "I wasn't the least bit interested, but my friend Lee was. She dragged me with her because she didn't want to go alone."

Sunny knew she had found something important from the first moment. Master Young P. Choi and his brother Joon P. Choi, founders and chief instructors at the Oriental Martial Arts College, were clearly exceptional teachers, interested in helping all their students, male and female. And Sunny realized that fighting skills were exactly what she needed in order to deal with the threat of violence against women, which had so undermined her spirit. In fact, it seemed to Sunny that the martial arts were almost an extension of feminism, so well did they fit in with the goals of strength, self-reliance, self-definition, and pride. And since she was limber and well coordinated, it was clear from the start that she was going to be good.

"I went in strictly for self-defense," she says. "I wasn't interested in anything but the fighting skills. But once I got involved, I fell in love with the martial arts—the beauty, the philosophy, the sport. I really grew, and I wanted to explore the martial arts in all their aspects."

The Oriental Martial Arts College offered training in *ship pal gi,* a hard style of kung fu, as well as tae kwon do. Sunny chose the kung fu classes simply because those were the ones her friend Lee joined.

"But when I saw the kung fu forms I was really hooked. The movements, the animal quality of them—I just couldn't get over it. When Master Young Choi, who was my kung fu instructor, did a crane form, or a tiger form, he was that animal. To this day, watching him work brings tears to my eyes. He is awe-inspiring."

In *ship pal gi,* beginners learn complex forms right away. "Then you just keep working on them," Sunny explains. "You do them over and over and over again. You can keep working on them forever. You learn to feel the flow, to get in touch with movement, and to let the movement take over. The form takes on a life of its own and it becomes a new part of you."

Sunny's flexibility enabled her to learn most of the moves easily. She practiced several times a week and within a few months, her forms were excellent. But she wasn't learning how to fight.

"That's when I began to pay more attention to tae kwon do. It seemed to me that I would learn more about fighting in those classes, so that was where I went. I loved the kung fu forms, but I wanted the fighting skills even more."

Sunny began to come to school early and to stay late so she could work on the punching bag without being observed. "If I thought

Sunny demonstrates the praying mantis strike to the face, a kung fu strike.

The clawing motion that can be used to strike an opponent's eyes following a praying mantis strike to the face.

anyone was watching, I just couldn't do it," she recalls. "I felt very awkward as a fighter, and found it very hard to be aggressive on a physical plane. If anyone was watching, I froze. My mind went blank and I couldn't think of anything to do. I learned the techniques easily enough. I was extremely limber and even the most difficult kicks were not hard for me. But it was very hard to overcome my self-consciousness and really get into the fight."

The attitudes of the male students added to the problem. Most of them did not take her seriously. "If your partners don't take you seriously," she explains, "it's awfully hard to feel legitimate. And if you don't feel legitimate, you keep putting your energy into apologizing, and you can't focus on developing skill. My partners were constantly asking me if I was all right, which was very demeaning. They turned away when it was time to choose partners and in a hundred other ways made it clear that they didn't think I really belonged there."

Sunny was determined. "I wanted those fighting skills badly, and I just wasn't going to let them slip through my fingers."

Encouraged by her instructors, who treated her with the same consideration they showed their male students, Sunny's skills grew. She lost her self-consciousness and stopped apologizing to her sparring partners. Most of them soon followed the teachers' example and treated her with respect.

Sunny's feelings of helplessness lifted. She devoted herself whole-heartedly to the Rape Crisis Center, now renamed the Toni Goman Feminist Rape Crisis Center, recruiting the staff, establishing the counseling service, representing the group to the community and to the media, coordinating the seventy volunteers who staffed the twenty-four-hour telephone line. At the same time, she continued with her job in the Columbus courts, and she continued to train as hard as she could, sometimes daily, in tae kwon do. In a little over a year, she was an advanced student. She began to teach new students and bought a lifetime membership in the Martial Arts

Sunny uses her lead hand to knock down her partner's front-hand block, thus opening her chest area as a target for a punch.

College with the money she saved by giving up her three-pack-a-day cigarette habit. She had also entered her first fighting competition. "It was totally unlike any sparring I'd ever done. I was in and out in thirty seconds. I didn't know what hit me!"

In the spring, WAR members learned that a National Center for the Prevention and Control of Rape had been created in Washington, D.C. It was a clearinghouse for funds, and granted money to groups working in the field of rape prevention. WAR decided to apply for a grant. Sunny had high hopes for it.

"Several of us, including me, were feeling burned out by crisis work. We felt like we were mopping up after the fact and never had a chance to develop any long-term goals. A grant would give us a chance to work on prevention and come up with strategies for long-term change."

Sunny applied to law school, too, in the hope of beginning in the fall. But because of her poor college record, she was placed on the waiting list "near the bottom." Restless and eager to begin something new, she was delighted when her brother invited her to join him on an all-summer trip to Asia. She rented her apartment, sold her car, got her passport, and quit her job. Then the trip fell through.

"I'd had it," Sunny says. "I just had to go somewhere. So I packed my bag and got on the road to hitchhike with no destination in mind at all—and it was just wonderful. I made it all the way down to Guatemala and I was on my way around the world with some women I had met from Michigan when I got the wire that WAR had been funded. We had gotten the grant! So I turned around and came back."

Once in Columbus again, Sunny visited the dean of the law school in person. "I told him they would have to let me study," she says. "I said they could keep me on the waiting list, but that I was going to come to classes and do the assignments anyway. I just knew that someone was going to drop out—someone always does—and I told him that when they did, I would be ready, course work prepared and money in hand!"

The dean agreed to let Sunny enroll officially.

"It was the best educational experience of my life," she says. "I loved it. I felt as though I was being let in on all the secrets of how things are done in this country, and I worked very hard. After all, I had pushed my way in and I was at the bottom of the class. By the end of the year, I was number one!"

By the end of the year, she had also organized self-defense classes for women law students and initiated a self-defense program as part of the WAR project.

"When I think about it now," she says, "I realize that the self-defense I taught came from being a feminist as much as from being a martial artist, because in self-defense, especially for women, the attitude is the important thing—the willingness to fight back, the belief that you should and that you can. Women are not brought up to think that way. We are brought up to give way to force immediately. There is no 'womanly art of self-defense.' If we're attacked, that's it! Perfect victims!"

Before beginning to teach self-defense, Sunny agonized over methods, techniques, procedures. But once she got started, she found it was easy. "The women were starved for information," she says, "and it didn't matter much what specific techniques you taught. What they needed first of all was a belief in their own bodies and in the fact that they were strong and resilient and could fight. If you could convey that, the rest was easy."

How did Sunny manage to work full time for WAR and earn top grades as a full-time law student too? "I could never have done it if not for the fact that I was also training in a martial art. Most people think they can't train because they have so many other things to do. But I think it works the other way. The more I trained, the more energy I had for everything!"

In 1977, with one year in law school behind her and two more to go, Sunny entered her first tournament fight as a black belt. There were still very few women competitors at that time, and they were not divided into classes based on size or weight, the way men were. Sunny, 5'5" and 115 pounds, had to fight a woman who was head and shoulders taller and almost twice as heavy. "The audience really got into it," she remembers. "I was clearly the underdog and they cheered and yelled for me. I felt like Rocky! And I won! It was great!"

After that, there was no stopping her. While she continued her studies in law school and her work with WAR's special project, she became a national competitor of the highest standing. "It's very exciting to be in a ring and to put into practice what you've been learning," she says. "It's as much a discipline and an exercise for the mind as it is for the body, maybe more so, because the only way to fight is with a calm mind. If you're angry or afraid, your reactions are slower. If you have to stop to think about what you're going to do, you get hit. For me, the most exciting thing about fighting is that feeling, that way of being so calm you can just let the skills take over. They just come out of you. The first time I ever went from a hook kick directly into a roundhouse kick was in a competition. Suddenly, it was just there and it worked perfectly. It's moments like that that make it so exciting."

Sunny's most dependable technique is her ax kick, a back leg kick that goes straight up and comes straight down on her opponent's head. "It's a great kick," she says. "There's just no getting away from it. It's incredibly powerful as well. It always works."

In 1978, Sunny entered the National AAU Tae Kwon Do Championships in Washington, D.C. She won her first gold medal and her first title: National AAU Champion, Bantam weight division.

Two months later, Sunny was invited to be on the first AAU women's tae kwon do team ever organized, and to participate in the upcoming pre-World Games in Seoul, Korea. Because the AAU was not providing travel money for the women's team, the Women's Action Collective in Columbus ran a fund-raising campaign to pay for Sunny's trip. She returned with a bronze medal.

Later that year, Sunny started her own branch of the Oriental Martial Arts College. It was for women only and it was called Feminists in Self-Defense Training: FIST.

"I started FIST because I think that many of the needs women have are not being met in traditional martial arts schools," Sunny says. "Not even in the best of them. Women have an aversion to violence and physical force in general, probably because of our history as a people subject to random violence. That aversion is very hard to overcome and it has to be addressed during training.

Sunny's ax kick about to fall. This is the kick she scores with most consistently. It is very difficult to block since it uses the entire length of the leg and has the force of gravity on its side. Sunny is one of the few people with enough flexibility to be able to use it in close as well as from a distance.

Traditional schools just don't do that. But most of all, I don't think women can learn self-defense without a feminist orientation to back them up. We have terrible struggles when it comes to defending ourselves, and those struggles don't go away when we learn a physical technique. Self-respect and the belief that we have the

left top: *A low roundhouse kick, the bread-and-butter kick of AAU tae kwon do competition. Sunny generally follows it with a quick switch of feet and a right leg ax kick.*

right to defend ourselves have to be written into the curriculum. Women aren't going to get it otherwise. And it has to be taught by strong women teachers who can be models and examples. It cannot be taught to women by men."

In 1979, Sunny graduated from law school and was admitted to the Ohio bar. She also won her second gold medal and her second National AAU Tae Kwon Do Championship. She was named captain of the AAU Women's Tae Kwon Do team, and Outstanding Female Taekwondoist of the Year 1979 by the National AAU Tae Kwon Do Committee. In July of the same year, she won her third gold medal and the title of World Champion when she fought and won at the World Invitational Tae Kwon Do Championships in Taiwan.

In 1981, Sunny won the National AAU Championship for the third time, and was selected Outstanding Female Taekwondoist of the Year for the second time.

In 1982, she won the national championship for the fourth time, and she was invited to represent the United States in the Pan American Tae Kwon Do Games held in Puerto Rico in December. It was the first time women were invited to participate. Sunny began her training regimen in September. She rose daily at six, and before going to her office, worked for an hour on the punching bag she installed in her garage, accompanied by a tape of reggae music by Jimmy Cliff and Bob Marley.

"Numbers get me through," she says, describing her routine: 150 front snap kicks, 150 roundhouse kicks, 200 power kicks—

left bottom: *A side snap kick to the face. Side kicks use the thrust of the hips for power. The edge of the heel is the striking surface.*

"slugging the bag as hard as I can"—in sets of 20, 100 with each foot; then 100 reverse punches, 100 front punches, and 100 combinations.

On her lunch hour, she worked out at the YWCA, sometimes with the punching bag, but more often delivering techniques to the X-rays she collected from a local hospital and taped to the wall. "They make a nice snap when you hit them right," she explains. "That's good immediate feedback."

At night, she worked for about two hours at the Martial Arts College. Equipped with chest protectors and padding, she and her partner concentrated on moving kicks for timing, and on techniques to use in response to attacks from others.

On Saturdays and Sundays, she focused entirely on training for competition, fighting timed rounds, one immediately after the other, all morning and all afternoon. Other students and her teachers observed her matches and offered their criticism on "just about everything."

"I had to pay a lot of extra attention to power," Sunny says. "In particular my low roundhouse kicks weren't focused properly and I wasn't getting the drive that should be in them. I had to reposition the leg I was pivoting on so I could get more power going through it and through the other person. I must have drilled that kick five billion times!"

Sunny returned from Puerto Rico with her sixth gold medal and now considers herself in semi-retirement. She has begun to coach, and she would like to do more coaching in the future and to promote women in international events. She wants to see more women in the martial arts, but for her, the feminist context is essential. Women who have experienced the combination, she says, will be able to do almost anything. Sunny herself, who has just been awarded a two-year, all-expenses-paid scholarship to study international and comparative law at Columbia University and at a university in Germany, is her own best example.

Kendo

KENDO IS THE MODERN ART OF JAPANESE SWORDFIGHTING. IT IS BASED ON the art of the samurai, but the sword, called a *shinai*, is made of bamboo, not steel, and fighters are well protected by padded, wired head gear, and coverings for the arms, chest, hips, and groin. You can lose a kendo match and still keep your head.

Kendo is safe, yet true to the form of real samurai sword-fighting. Strikes are full force and powerful. They are directed at the vital, vulnerable parts of opponents' bodies. They are accompanied by *kiais*, the louder and more spirited the better. A kendo meet is full of explosive action—bodies lunge and crash, *shinais* strike with great power, wild battle cries come from everywhere.

Kenjutsu, the art on which kendo is based, flourished in the days of feudal Japan, when warlords battled for land and power. Their warriors, called *bushi* or samurai, were raised to fight, taught that their lives belonged to the lords they served, and bound by the code of *Bushido*, "the way of the warrior," in which loyalty, courage, and honor were more important than life itself. "The way of the warrior is death," was a maxim.

Immersed in Zen Buddhism, which taught them not to look back once their course of action was decided, Japanese warriors were not afraid to die or reluctant to kill on or off the battlefield. "A bushi

119

is not to be interfered with in cutting down a fellow who has behaved badly toward him" said a feudal code that gave *bushi* the right of "killing and going away." Their skills were fierce, their spirit imperturbable, their weapons ferocious. And first among them was the sword.

The samurai sword had a single-edged, curved steel blade almost three feet long and about one and one-quarter inches wide, one-quarter inch thick at the back, and tapering evenly to a razor edge in front. It was meant to be held with both hands. The family crest was usually carved on the scabbard, the standard color of which was black with a tinge of red or green. The samurai sword was a powerful weapon and an important symbol of honor, dignity, and ancestry.

Swordfighting, too, was more than a physical contest. It was the arena in which to develop a strong, brave, virtuous soul. Miyamoto Musashi (1584-1645), the greatest swordfighter in Japanese history, who won his first duel at the age of thirteen, saw the sword not as an "instrument of death" but as an "instrument for the development of spiritual perfection." "The sword and the soul are one," said a proverb.

Samurai developed new methods and styles of swordfighting almost continuously. At one point in the 1600s, close to two thousand styles were in active use. In the 1700s peace came to Japan, but *kenjutsu* remained a very popular art. To make it safer to learn, steel swords were replaced by wooden swords called *bokken.* The *bokken,* in turn, was replaced by the even lighter and safer bamboo *shinai.* Protective body gear was introduced, and *kenjutsu* was renamed *kendo,* to indicate that it was no longer concerned exclusively with combat but with the strengths and virtues combat often inspires. Its value was in the spirit of the fight and the fighter, not in the blade or the outcome of the contest.

Kendo is still popular throughout Japan, where it is taught in the public schools as well as in private clubs. In the United States, it has long been practiced in the Japanese-American communities of the West Coast, and in the past fifteen years, it has begun to attract followers in other parts of the country as well. Today American *kenshi* (kendo players) make up a small but enthusiastic group numbering somewhere under two thousand. Of these, about forty are women. Valerie Eads is one of them.

VALERIE EADS

A s soon as I heard their yells and saw them step in to attack, I knew this was for me," says Valerie Eads, one of the few American women who practices kendo, the Japanese "way of the sword." "There was no letup. They were flying around the room, masked, padded, black pants billowing, bashing each other over the head and shrieking. I couldn't wait to try it."

Valerie was talking in the Office of Medieval Studies at New York's City University Graduate Center, where she is researching the life of the Countess Matilda, a woman who wielded great power in eleventh-century Europe. Valerie had found her way to the New York Buddhist Academy Kendo Club in 1972, because she was looking for a sport, something strenuous and demanding to do on a regular basis. She had been a ballet student for almost ten years, and she knew the value and fun of disciplined exercise.

There were few other women in the club at the time, but that didn't phase Valerie in the least. Born in Missouri and raised in Philadelphia by her grandmother, she has always gone her own way, never quite fitting in with any crowd, never afraid to make waves.

"Childhood and adolescence were the pits," she says, recalling how she quit high school out of boredom, wandering from one job

123

to another, earning the lowest wage employers were allowed to pay in 1958—one dollar an hour—and finally going back because even school was better than working. But she continued to be indifferent to classes, grades, friends, and social pressure, spending all her time with a group of bikers—"older men in their twenties"—who lived for their motorcycles as much as she lived for hers. She didn't quite fit in with them, of course, but even less did she fit in with the Motor Maids of America, women bikers who invited Valerie to ride with them after seeing her at races.

"They were very proper and ladylike," Valerie recalls, "probably to compensate for their unladylike love of motorcycles. But I wasn't a lady at all, and they took their invitation back on the same day they gave it to me."

Graduating from high school at the bottom of her class, but at the very top of the group of students from all over America who took the College Board Examinations, Valerie was offered a full scholarship to attend Temple University. She majored in literature, but put it to one side when she discovered the Pennsylvania Ballet.

"Once I started to study," she says, "ballet became the center of my life. I would have left college except for the fact that my scholarship was my only means of support. I thought of going to school as my job. It kept me in pocket money so I could study ballet."

At nineteen, Valerie was old to be starting as a dancer. And at 5′7″ and 130 pounds, she was heavy by the standards of contemporary ballet. Nevertheless, she studied throughout her college years, and for four years after graduation she traveled back and forth between New York, where she studied at Richard Thomas's School of Ballet, and Philadelphia, where she lived. She appeared in the productions of several small ballet companies, but by 1970, when she moved to New York for good, it had become clear to her that she wasn't going to "get anywhere" in dance.

"Rationally, I guess I knew it all the time," she says. "I knew I had started too late, and I knew I was too heavy. But there was always some small part of me that kept hoping. Then in 1969 I injured my hip, and I was out of the studio for weeks at a time. That was the last straw. I didn't want to, but I had to admit that I didn't have a future as a dancer."

Valerie turned for a while to the theatre, playing in summer stock and working with an experimental off-Broadway company. But for her, theater was a poor second to the world of dance. And with the women's movement, and the new ideas about women making more and more of an impression on her, Valerie was less and less inclined to accept the roles that were available.

"When I first heard about the women's movement," she says, "I thought it was ridiculous, and that it had nothing to do with me. I had already come to terms with the fact that women had no status and no respect in the world. All those Saturday afternoons at the movies watching Maureen O'Hara cry and hide behind John Wayne had gotten their message across and I had as much con- tempt for women as any man. So when I first heard about a 'women's movement' I couldn't have been less interested. But somewhere along the way I realized that I had just accepted the cultural 'line' about women—and that that line was what the women's movement was beginning to identify and fight against. When I was offered roles that reinforced the stereotype of women as emotional wrecks who needed men to give them a reason for living, I did not want to play them. When I tried to discuss the problem with my director and got a 'so what?' I knew it was time to make my exit."

Valerie had taken up aikido when she stopped dancing, having heard that it was a good martial art for people with training in classical dance. But she didn't get very far, mostly, she thinks, because of the school in which she was enrolled. The instructor didn't seem interested in teaching, and he was certainly not in- terested in teaching women.

"It was the custom for people to teach a class after being promoted to black belt," she recalls. "It was part of the ritual of promotion itself. But this instructor wouldn't let women black belts teach. He said it wouldn't 'look good.' "

After almost two years, Valerie lost interest entirely, and wondered whether or not to try another martial art. Word was out about the problems women were having with the instructors in karate schools. Then a friend from the aikido class invited her to visit the New York Buddhist Academy Kendo Club.

"That was it," she says now. "All that screaming and bashing of heads was definitely for me."

The assistant instructor at the club, *Sensei* Kanichi Ishizuka, was someone Valerie was delighted to find, a man whose respect for his students was always clear and whose manner was always encouraging.

"He was a great guy," Valerie wrote later, "a teacher who had infinite patience with beginners no matter how heavy handed or inept. No matter how down anyone was, Ishizuka *Sensei* could make them feel they had done at least something right that day."

Valerie worked well with him, although her manner—straightforward and without a hint of deference—offended some of the male students. "At first I tried to get my *kiai* low, so no one would be able to tell I was a woman," Valerie recalls. "With all the gear you wear in kendo, anyone can be anything. But after a while, I *kiai*'d naturally. I wanted my opponents to know whom they were being clobbered by!"

In kendo, students wear the same *gi* jackets used in most other martial arts, but a distinctive skirtlike trouser called a *hakama*, instead of the usual *gi* pants. The *hakama* is traditional male attire in Japan. It was the clothing of the nobility and of the samurai. *Kenshi* (kendo players) also wear protective armor: the *do*, a shield for the chest and ribs; the *tare*, an apronlike shield for the lower part of the body; the *men*, a face protector, similar to a catcher's mask;

*V*alerie (in white gi top) following through after a cut to men (her partner's head). Her shinai is recoiling, and she has begun to move forward with her left foot. Her partner, who has just attempted to block her strike, will probably follow through with a strike to do (Valerie's mid-section).

and the *kote*, thick padded gloves. Class procedure varies from school to school, but in most, students line up in order of rank and at a signal from the instructor, sit to meditate, placing the *men, kote* and *shinai* in carefully prescribed positions on the floor before them. At another signal from the instructor, meditation is over. Students put on their head gear and gloves. They bow and pick up their weapons.

"You never just grab it and get up," Valerie says. "There is a certain way to handle it and that's part of the art."

The students pair off and practice basics. They may do as many as four hundred strikes and double-time strikes to targets announced by the instructor. They may then jog for ten minutes or so, then practice turning, moving sideways, forward, and back.

After basics is *keiko*—sparring, or free-fighting, as it is sometimes called. Students pair off, bow, and "go to war." That is what Valerie saw when she observed a class. But as she found when she decided to study kendo, beginners don't engage in *keiko* at all. They spend the first few months just learning how to handle the *shinai*, how to hold it, how to swing it, how to get it to hit specified targets (called "cuts").

"In my school, new beginners stood on the side and advanced people came to us," Valerie explains. "They stood in front of us for a minute and gave us a chance to swing the *shinai*. They were just targets, they didn't engage us at all. We didn't even wear our *men*. After a few weeks, we left the beginner's area and found our own targets on the floor—someone who had finished a match and hadn't begun another yet. We would run over, bow, and strike. Then we'd move on to someone else. I found this part of the training very boring, but it does teach you how to use the *shinai*, something which feels totally unnatural at first. It's very hard to develop any judgment about distance, to know where to stand in order to get your strike in. And even though it's boring, you are in constant motion and that in itself builds endurance."

In the beginning, exploring her powers of endurance was more than enough to keep Valerie going. "There were no limits to the demands made on you," she recalls. "No one would ever tell you to slow down. It was always 'do more! do more!' And every time I came out of class I found that I *could* do more. Even after all those years in ballet, I was discovering muscles I didn't know I had. I loved the experience of being so tired my knees were wobbling— and suddenly finding a new reserve of strength. You learn a new kind of hardiness, a new idea of your own potential."

After about three months, Valerie was allowed to put on full armor and join in *keiko*. Her natural aggression was her greatest gift. "I never lacked that, and in kendo it was an important plus. If you really don't have the urge to nail somebody, I think it would be hard to get involved."

Kendo was fun, challenging, hard, and exciting. Its history was intriguing to Valerie, too. She learned that women born into the warrior classes of feudal Japan—when swordfighting was in its heyday—often learned to fight. They were expected to be adept users of the *naginata*, a long spear with a curved blade, and the *tanto*, a dagger, and many women also learned to use the single-edged long sword, the prototype for the weapon used in modern kendo. Several Japanese women had made their way into battle and onto the pages of history as courageous and skillful warriors. In extreme situations, it seemed, social class could be more important than gender in determining what you were allowed to do. In rigidly organized class societies, women sometimes had opportunities that were "out of role" and quite extraordinary. That seemed to have been the case in feudal Japan. Had there been parallels in European history, women of rank who had been warriors and military commanders in their own right? Valerie began to read on her own and to think about going back to school to study medieval European history.

At about this time, Valerie ran into a woman she had met in AFTRA, the TV and radio performers' union. Joan Shigekawa, a producer, was working on a TV pilot for a series in which public television had expressed interest. It was to be called "Woman Alive!" and it would explore the lives of important and unusual women. Would Valerie be willing to help Joan put the pilot together?

"I was delighted," Valerie says. "I was dangling then and looking for something to do. This was important and it could be fun."

Ms. Magazine donated office space to Joan and her crew. One afternoon, Valerie had occasion to call *Black Belt Magazine*, one of the best known martial arts magazines. Its coverage of women, Valerie thought, was awful.

"There wasn't *enough* coverage, for one thing," she says. "And the coverage they had was of the cutesy-pie school—'Karate Kutie

Kicks Up a Ruckus' kind of thing. I called to ask for statistics for Joan and in the course of the conversation I did some griping about the magazine's coverage of women. I said I thought there should be a regular column to deal with women in the martial arts and the editor, Bob McLaughlin, said if I thought so I should go ahead and write one. So I did!"

Valerie called her column "Fighting Woman" and for it she wrote essays about the things she thought needed airing.

"The principles of *budo* [the martial arts] have always been seen as universal," she wrote in 1974, in her first column, explaining why a women's column should be written at all. "The martial arts have survived the mechanization of warfare, cross-cultural transmission, the American occupation, and crass commercialization. For some reason, it seems that a lot of people don't feel that the arts can survive the women's movement."

The arrival of large numbers of women into the schools "should be nothing more than a statistic," she noted, but unfortunately that was not the case. Many men, including male teachers, thought women had no business in the arts at all. "When the martial arts have recovered from the arrival of the women," she wrote, "this column will probably die a natural death."

In the issues that followed, Valerie's articles ranged from "Women's Judo" to "Sex in the Dojo," "The Best Him vs. The Best Her," and "Why Women Can't Fight."

"Fighting as such symbolizes everything a woman has been taught not to be," she wrote. "They find it hard to do, even in their own defense, because they are taught, from cradle to split-level, that they can't."

In an article criticizing the AAU for its unfair policies toward women athletes, Valerie urged women to go to meetings and make their voices heard. "Remember," she wrote, "that if you don't do it for yourself, there is always someone who is only too happy to do it for you—*his* way."

Valerie wrote feature articles for *Black Belt,* too, and for other magazines as well, including *The Deadly Hands of Kung Fu, Black Sports, Fighting Arts, Self-Defense World, Karate Illustrated, World Karate,* and *Seventeen.* She continued her "Fighting Woman" column for two years before she quit "by mutual agreement." A beautifully produced and written magazine called *Black Belt Woman* had just made its debut, but there was nevertheless plenty of audience for the informal newsletter Valerie wanted to start when she left *Black Belt Magazine.* Taking her title with her, she called it *Fighting Woman News.*

"I had absolutely no idea how to go about something like that," she says. "I had no money either, which was probably just as well, because I would have lost it all."

For the first issue, she had a paid subscription list of twenty people, a budget of sixty-five dollars, and a dedicated staff of one. But it was crammed with news of women in the various arts, tournaments, championships, meetings, debates, discussions, progress, frustrations, reviews of products, and reviews of books. Valerie did not pull any punches.

"Women are considered only along with the handicapped," she wrote of a how-to book, which had been widely praised in the national magazines. "It doesn't say much about women, which may be good considering what is usually said," she wrote when reviewing another book.

Valerie didn't try to maintain a tight production schedule. She brought out issues as often as they could be gotten together. "This issue is a little late," she noted on one editorial page, "because our entire staff was out with the flu. It's hard to put out a newsletter without the publisher, editor, production staff, art director, copy person, or mail clerk. She's feeling better now."

In the winter of 1976, when other sports media were filled with articles about the Olympics and Olympic champions, *Fighting Woman News* urged a revival of the Heran Games, the ancient women's counterpart to the original Olympic games from which women had been barred entirely.

After noting the anti-woman discrimination in the modern International Olympic Committee, Valerie wrote, "It's long past due that the Olympic Games were replaced in the lives of female athletes with something more meaningful. Let's revive the Heran Games. Not for governments and businesses, but for women. All women, regardless of nationality or national sports committees. Not for the glory of nations but to celebrate the beauty and skill of women. Wasn't that supposed to be the Olympic idea in the first place?"

A few months later, Valerie's teacher, Kanichi Ishizuka, died.

"Like all the members of our kendo club, I cried my eyes out at his funeral," she wrote in an article for *Black Belt Woman,* recalling the trip the club had made to Toronto the year before for a kendo competition. "For me it was my first, for him the last."

Twenty-one people from the club had signed up to go, which meant that there was one 'odd person out' when it came to assigning rommates. "Guess who it was," Valerie wrote. "The one other woman player doubled with her husband. That left me to go solo or triple up with two guys. Whether they were afraid to be assaulted or not assaulted, I don't know," she added, "but I was assigned a single room without being asked. Talk about feeling rejected. I griped about the cost, but no one took the hint."

In Toronto, at the check-in desk, Valerie was still griping. " 'Twenty-three bucks!' I said out loud to whomever was within hearing. 'I don't spend that much in a week!' Then a soft voice said, 'Twenty-three dollars? That's ridiculous! Why don't you come in with us?' It was Ishizuka *Sensei.* He told the desk clerk to scratch the single and make his room a triple and off we went, Ishizuka, fifth-degree black belt, Shibata, fourth-degree, and Eads, beginner.

"Of all the people in that club, Ishizuka was the only one who knew or cared that I might have the same motivation as anyone else for wanting to share a hotel room," she wrote. "He realized that even though I was a woman, I was a human being."

Valerie had learned a great deal under Ishizuka's tutelage. When she began kendo, she felt like a "ten year old let loose in an amusement park." But she had since become a refined, controlled player.

"I learned not to play myself into the ground," she says. "Kendo is loud and furious and all the other things I liked about it when I first saw it, but it's also timing, strategy, focus, and above all coordination. For example, you have to strike your target with only a certain part of the *shinai,* the part that extends from the point to about ten inches up. That's called the cutting edge. If you land with any other portion, it doesn't count, it's not a valid hit, because that's not the cutting edge of a real sword. And the hit has to have real force. It has to convince the observer that if it had been made with a real sword in a real fight, it would have killed or disabled your opponent. And, for the strike to be proper, your right foot has to hit the ground at the same instant that your cutting edge lands on your target, so that body and sword are together. If your foot is off the ground when the strike lands, your coordination is off, your body weight is not in the strike, and in a scored match you would get no point, even though you landed on target. Your *kiai* has to come out at the exact right instant too, the instant of contact, to show that not only did you get your target, but you know you got it. Contact alone isn't enough. That's just people beating on each other with sticks."

Valerie has begun to focus on footwork lately, agreeing, as an older player put it, that "making cuts with your hands" is only the first level on which kendo can be played. "We were about to begin a match," Valerie recalls, "and I was explaining that I couldn't use my right arm because of an injury, and he said, 'So what? You don't need your right arm! Only beginners play with their hands!

Your attack must be in your footwork. As a master, you will attack with your spirit!' "

She is working out the footwork involved in setting up secondary targets. "I will go for *kote*," she explains, "but even as I move, I am setting up for a second attack to *do*—which I will use if, for example, my opponent dips out of range and attempts to counter my first attack. What I'm doing is a fake in a way, but it's also real—the first strike has to come at your opponent strong enough to make them move. If they don't move, they get it. If they do move, they get the second hit. And in kendo, a good strike hits like a brick. If you're hit, you really know it."

Late in the spring, some months after *Sensei* Ishizuka's death, Valerie attended the Third World Kendo Championships in London, organized by the International Kendo Federation. Although a competent *kenshi,* she was not good enough to compete in the world championships. She hoped instead to play in the good will tournament scheduled before the main event. Such tournaments are usually held before championship contests in order to give lesser players a chance to participate. There are no prizes other than modest trophies in such tournaments, but players are divided according to rank so the matches can be roughly between equals. When Valerie saw the schedule however, she was puzzled. Players were asked to register in one of six divisions. Divisions one through four were for players of all the different ranks, from lowest (Division One) to highest (Division Four). But Divisions Five and Six were for "Ladies" and "Youth."

The head of Valerie's school first told her that the Ladies Division was an option for women who wished to play only against other women. Valerie could, if she chose, register for one of the ranked divisions. But when she did, he called her out and said he had been wrong. She would have to play in the Ladies Division after all. It was against the rules, he said, for women to compete against men.

Unhappy but resigned, Valerie entered and played in the Ladies

At the end of each match, players bow to one another before leaving the floor. The player on the right has just been tested for promotion. Valerie was his partner. Examiners are at the table.

Division, only to learn afterwards that no such rule existed. There were women competing against men in the world championship itself. Her instructor had lied. When the championships were over and the teams had gone home, much of Valerie's enthusiasm was gone, too.

"I really felt like a fool," Valerie says. "Having been lied to and kept out of competition. I might have dropped out of kendo entirely, but by that time I knew about a lot of other women in other martial arts who had been through things that were much worse. Knowing about them helped a lot, and though I didn't have much heart for training, I didn't stop completely."

Nevertheless, her enthusiasm was dampened, and for a while her training was sporadic. Restless and not sure of where it would lead, she decided to go back to school for a master's degree in Medieval and Renaissance Studies. The City University of New York accepted her in its graduate program and she set to work.

The following year, things picked up in kendo when a man

named Mozart Ishizuka (no relation to Valerie's original teacher) made his presence felt in New York.

"He impressed me as a very conservative person when I first met him," Valerie says, laughing. "One of the most erroneous impressions I ever got. He turned out to be the maverick of the kendo world. He was a senior student at my school and had always stayed pretty much in the background. But once he got moving, things began to happen all along the East Coast."

Kendo was already organized into a federation on the West Coast. Ishizuka thought there might be enough interest to warrant an East Coast federation. He contacted local Y's, schools, and other groups in the Japanese-American community, since that was where the main interest in kendo could be found, and set up kendo classes wherever there was a gym.

"Once he got a kind of word-of-mouth network going, especially in the Japanese-American business community, lots of people began turning up," Valerie says. "There were former kendo players and would-be kendo players in all sorts of places—people who had played in college, or in their community in Japan, and who never even thought about playing in America, but were very interested once there was a place to do it."

One person who came out of the business community, a man who had been an active and honored *kenshi* in Japan, was Kunimitsu Kaizuka. He became Valerie's second important teacher.

"He never thought he'd play kendo in America," Valerie remembers. "He had to send to Japan for his gear. He was astonishing! Small, with wire glasses, about as polite and correct as a person can be. But once he put on his gear and picked up his *shinai*, he was utterly and completely transformed. It was like watching Clark Kent go into the dressing room and seeing Superman come charging out!"

Ishizuka asked Valerie to work with him on extending the kendo network. He asked her to be a member of the board of directors of the new federation, and to serve as its executive secretary.

Did this mean that women in the Eastern Federation would be eligible to participate in tournaments and events of all kinds without being discriminated against in any way?

"Trust me," Valerie says with a smile. "I wrote the constitution. It's largely based on the national constitution, which has always allowed women on teams, but in ours the principle of open competition is even clearer and more emphatic."

Though Valerie has and would fight again for the principle of open competition, she doesn't consider herself a good competitor. She enters tournaments for fun. She enjoys testing her skills, and she enjoys the interchange of a lively match. She is now incorporating in her game the principles of coordination and timing, which are the heart of kendo, and is enjoying it more than ever.

"There seems to be no end of interesting problems to deal with on the floor," she says. "Opponents who are bigger and stronger are the least of it. It's the young, fast ones who are the real challenges. I played someone last week who only came up to my shoulders—but he just flew right by me!"

She is concentrating now on developing what is called a "strong point."

"The point of your *shinai* is your protection," she explains. "It stands between you and your opponent, a barrier and a point of communication. Beginners just charge and bash. But someone who can control the point is doing a different thing entirely. It's not so much physical strength as something psychological. You often see it in older players. They don't go charging around. Sometimes they just stand there, points crossed, but a lot is going on. If you look carefully you can see their points quivering. They're testing one another, looking for a break in concentration. That seems to be the main thing. It's an element of the weapon that I'm just beginning to explore, using the point to take control, communicating through it. It's enormously interesting."

Valerie and her partner jockey for position. Each tries to move backward without getting cut, at the same time preparing to deliver a cut.

The Eastern United States Kendo Federation is now going strong, with a membership upwards of three hundred, grand tournaments once a year, local meets, and events throughout the year. *Fighting Woman News* has stabilized too, with a subscription list of about one thousand. It is indexed in *Women Studies Abstracts*, considered suitable for library collections, and has become much more than the newsletter Valerie had in mind when she started it.

"It's become a record," she says, "a documented witness. Women's rights have been won and lost before, and I wouldn't be surprised if they were lost again. If they are, and if distorted ideas about women's nature and capacities are ever trotted out again as The Truth, I hope *Fighting Woman News* will help to show that they aren't. When people go poring through the archives, I want it to be one of the things they find, so that no one will be able to say 'women can't do that,' or 'women have never done that.' If some lone woman in some future time complains, people won't be able to say, 'no one ever complained about this before—what's the matter with *you?'* "

Valerie herself has been promoted to second-degree black belt, earned her master of arts degree in Medieval and Renaissance Studies, and is now immersed in Latin documents, artillery maps, the chronicles of monks, and the courses she needs for her Ph.D. The research she is doing on Matilda was suggested by one of her professors, but her work is not a school requirement. Valerie is pursuing it on her own.

"Matilda was one of the greatest lords of her century," she says. "She controlled more land than William the Conqueror, and she was a brilliant strategist, a better general than any of them. Yet you almost never hear about her. When she's mentioned in the books at all, she's described as a religious fanatic—but the people of her own time described her with adjectives like the Latin *invictissime,* which means 'most invincible' and *bellipotens,* which means 'mighty in war!' "

If Matilda had been a man, Valerie believes, she would have been given a much more prominent place in history, and we would all be familiar with her.

"Sometimes I think I'd like to rewrite all the history books and put in everything that was left out, fill in all the blank spots where women should be. Part of the reason women are absent from history is that women have not been the ones to write the official versions of anything," says the editor and publisher of *Fighting Woman News* and the woman who wrote the constitution of the Eastern U.S. Kendo Federation. "Until now."

Aikido

AIKIDO IS THE MARTIAL ART IN WHICH YOU LEARN TO DEFEND YOURSELF without harming your attacker. It has been called the "ultimate" self-defense system because it is entirely and exclusively defensive. The ethical intention to cause no harm is as essential to aikido as the physical skills that make it possible.

Aikido moves are almost always circular, revolving around your center of gravity. You don't grapple with your attacker. Instead, you learn to turn "like a door on a hinge" to get out of the line of attack, take control of the force directed against you, and use it to lead your opponent where you want her to go. The force of her own attack propels her. You also learn to apply joint-locking techniques, which immobilize but do not have to harm your opponent.

The syllable *ai* in aikido means harmony, and aikido is based on a belief in the harmony of the universe, the idea that everything fits together and works together to make one orderly, beautiful whole. Violent forces disrupt the harmonious flow of things and have to be "neutralized." When you use aikido techniques to defend yourself, you are working to restore the harmony of the universe. Aikidoists don't talk in terms of "winning a fight." They talk about "peaceful reconciliation."

As important as the belief in harmony is the belief in internal energy—*ki*, the middle syllable in aikido—sometimes said to be the essence of life itself. Everyone is born with *ki*. Babies use it naturally, when, for instance, without being aware of what they are doing, they close their fists so firmly that an adult can't force them open. Although adults have *ki* too, the ability to tap it and use it at will is usually lost. All the martial arts are concerned with gaining, or regaining, access to *ki*, but aikido stresses it from the outset. The power *ki* adds to one's movement is quite distinct from muscular, purely physical power.

Aikido, which has been called the most subtle and sophisticated of the martial arts, is relatively new. It was created in this century by Morihei Uyeshiba, one of the greatest Japanese martial artists of all time, a man who studied over two hundred arts and was a master of many of them. Uyeshiba intended his new art to be one that deepened and intensified the true meaning of the martial arts, a meaning that came to him "as if in a dream" after years of searching. By teaching us to defend ourselves from violent forces, he wrote, all the martial arts place us on the side of harmony. But if they overcome force with force, they themselves become disruptive. The highest art would be one that enabled us to defend ourselves from attack without making an attack of our own. It would be a way to overcome violence entirely by turning its disruptive energy into harmonious energy. Uyeshiba introduced aikido as a system that would do this.

"Aikido is not a technique to fight with or defeat the enemy," he wrote. "It is the way to reconcile the world and make human beings one family. The secret of aikido is to harmonize ourselves with the movement of the universe and bring ourselves into accord with the universe itself. He who has gained the secret of aikido has the universe in himself and can truly say, 'I am the universe.' "

BETH
AUSTIN

When Beth Austin went to her first class in aikido, no one took it seriously, least of all Beth herself. She was not an athlete and never had been. She had no interest in the martial arts or in self-defense, no special interest in any area of the struggle for women's rights. If someone had suggested that she would be a first-rate martial artist someday, she would probably have laughed. If they had suggested she would be a pioneer and a model for other women, she would have thought they were talking about someone else.

"I got started in aikido because the class cost next to nothing," Beth says, "and it looked like fun."

Beth had just arrived in California when she happened into the aikido class. It was offered by the company for which she was working as a data processor. That was the best job she had ever had and she was delighted with it. In fact, she was pleased with every aspect of her move to California. She felt that a new period of her life was beginning, and that the hard years were behind her.

"I was born and raised in Philadelphia," she says, "and my upbringing was very strict and very conventional. I was taught that if you obeyed the rules and did what you were told, you would be happy. I did, but I wasn't happy at all, and I thought there was something terribly wrong with me."

143

Beth expected to go to work after high school, to marry soon after that and then to settle down and raise a family of her own. And she did. She worked as a secretary after graduating from high school, got married, and a year later gave birth to a son, Kris Robert. Although everything seemed to be in order, in fact Beth was desperately unhappy. Her husband had a violent temper and soon after their marriage, he began to beat her. She was afraid to tell anyone and afraid to leave him. Finally, when Kris was eighteen months old, she fled with him to Denver, Colorado.

"I was afraid to go to my family, because that was the first place my husband would look for me," she says. "I had no special reason for going to Denver—except that it was far from Philadelphia and my husband would never think of looking for me there. It was also a state capital, so I thought I'd be able to find a job in an office without too much trouble. I realize now that it was a do-or-die situation I had created for myself, a situation of extreme crisis. But it was just what I needed to shake me out of my conditioning and set me on a whole new path."

Until that time, Beth feels she was "unformed" as an individual. She had lived the way she was expected to. But in Denver, she was on her own. Although it was frightening, she learned that she could think for herself, make her own decisions, manage her life and manage it well.

"Kris and I moved constantly when we first got there. I found a job as a secretary easily enough, but I couldn't earn much money. It was hard to find good people to take care of Kris, and it was hard to find a good place to live. When I look back on it now, I feel as though we grew together, Kris and I. Of course, he was a baby growing up and I was a young woman. But still, we were alone together and I think he taught me a lot."

After a few months, Beth was in touch with her family again, though it was years before she let them tell anyone at all where she was.

"They urged me to return to Philadelphia, which, of course, I couldn't do," she says. "And eventually, everything worked out. I found a woman who was in a similar situation—she had two daughters to raise—and we moved in together. One way or another, we managed. I have never regretted it, not for one second."

Beth worked as a secretary for several years, but she knew she needed better job skills if she was ever going to earn a decent salary. So when the state of Colorado established a training program for data processors—a new career field at that time—she enrolled. When the program was over, she made plans to move to California, where job opportunities seemed best. Within two weeks, she had found the highest-paying job she had ever had, as well as a large, sunny apartment and a good local school for Kris.

"I was very lucky," Beth says. "The company that hired me was exceptionally humane and ethical. It offered lots of programs and benefits to its employees. The aikido club, which started just after I got there, was offered during the lunch break in a beautiful recreation area at five dollars a month."

Beth didn't think of aikido as a sport or even as a fighting art when she began. It was a way of exercising that looked, if anything, playful and easy. She soon found out that it was neither.

"The turns, the falls, the throws, all the things that looked like so much fun weren't fun when you didn't know how to do them," she says. "And I couldn't get the hang of it at all. I thought I was a clutz—I *was* a clutz—and I didn't think I would ever have any strength or coordination. I was afraid of being thrown and I couldn't seem to fall without getting hurt. My body slammed down on the mat hard. I was always aching and sore."

Since the aikido club was brand new, there was a lot of organizational work to do, and members were expected to do it. At one of the first meetings when officers were elected, Beth was elected secretary and asked to take charge of the membership drive. It was

*B*eth demonstrates a kokynnage (momentum) throw with student Fritt Henley. In a momentum throw, the attacker's own energy is used to throw her down. In this case, Beth turned slightly out of the line of Fritt's attack, grabbed Fritt's left arm, turned in the direction Fritt was heading, lifted and then dropped her down.

this involvement, along with the interest and kindness of the club's elected president, which kept her going in the beginning.

"I was so bad, and it was so hard for me," she says, "that I would have quit any number of times. In fact, I did quit. But I kept going back because of the administrative jobs and because whenever I missed a few classes the president would come and ask me where I had been and urge me to come back again."

Slowly Beth began to develop the competence she had thought was beyond her. "By dint of practice alone, I was learning to relax, to roll with a fall, to spread out the impact so I wasn't just slamming onto the mat like a ton of bricks."

She also learned that physical skill is not all there is to aikido. "From the beginning, we talked about getting mind and body to work together, using our inner energy and using—trans-forming—the energy coming at us from our opponent, directing the force that already exists, leading it away from you. A technique may look right but be all wrong," she explains, "if you are doing it on the basis of muscular strength alone."

The philosophy behind aikido appealed to Beth too. "Aikido is totally nonviolent, which is hard for some people to understand. But you don't have to cause harm in order to protect yourself. A master never does. In fact, hurting your opponent is a sign that you are not in control and haven't mastered the technique. The more I came to understand this, the more I realized that aikido has immediate and obvious consequences for your entire life. It is a way to get in touch with your personal power, your ability to be in control of what happens to you, to express your power effectively, nonviolently."

By the time a year had gone by, though Beth was still at the beginner's level, she was asked to take part in demonstrations. At one of the first, she was in an exercise in which she and four other students were to rush up, grab their instructor, and try to throw him over.

"You have to be very careful in these exercises," she says, "because even though you know what everyone is going to do, the action is fast and bodies really go flying. I was rushing into the attack when the person in front of me was thrown very hard. His foot came up full force and clobbered me right in the middle of my chest. I heard the audience let out a loud collective gasp. I really felt that foot, but my training had taken over and I had turned a little so the blow was just slightly deflected. It was enough so that I was able to continue my attack without stopping at all. It was a good experience for the audience and for me, showing us all that with proper training, women can take it!"

At the time, 1971, aikido was still unknown to most Americans. Aikido students were urged to spread the word about it and introduce it to people whenever they could. Partly in that spirit, Beth volunteered to teach a self-defense course based on aikido techniques at the Venice, California, Women's Center.

"Aside from my genuine desire to spread the word, I volunteered for all the wrong reasons," she says. "I thought that I was
definitely second-rate, but that it didn't matter because I would
only be teaching women!"

Thirty women signed up for the course, many more than Beth
had expected. She had not been involved with the women's liberation movement and was not aware of the growing interest in
self-defense. Nor did she realize that her feeling of being second-
rate was common among women, no matter how competent they
were, and that this feeling had been the subject of a great deal of
recent discussion in women's groups.

Beth introduced herself to her students with a typical woman's
apology. "I'm not very good at this," she said, "but I'll teach you
what I know. Maybe later I'll get my instructor to come. In the
meantime, I'll do my best, even though—"

At this, one of the students stood up. "Wait a minute," she said
in a loud clear voice. "We didn't come here to hear this!"

Beth was dumbfounded.

"Look at you!" the woman said. "You're up there in a *gi*. You've
been training in a martial art! You have a lot to teach us—and we
want to learn from you." There was a rush of whispering among
the other women, and a lot of nodding of heads.

"I felt a wave of acceptance and affirmation so strong I was
almost overcome," Beth says. "It was the most positive thing I'd
ever experienced in my life. And suddenly I realized that what that
woman was saying was true. I did have a lot to teach them and I
wanted to, very much!"

After that class, Beth took herself seriously in a way she had
never been able to before. "For the first time, I was able to step
outside of myself and overcome my self-consciousness. I stopped
thinking of myself as a woman, and saw myself as a teacher
instead. I wasn't trying to prove myself—I was trying to share
something I had learned. It made all the difference in the world to

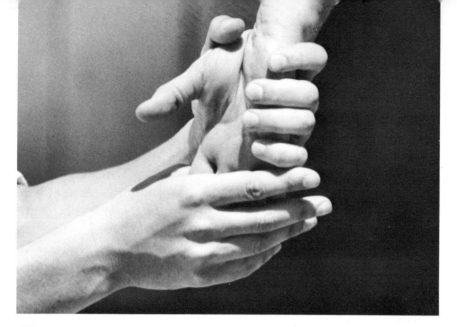

The sankyo *hold, used to control an attacker's movement. This hold locks the joints of the wrist, elbow, and shoulder; the arm thus becomes a lever, which can be used to move the entire body.*

me. I was able to get out of my own way and I really began to grow."

Nevertheless, as one of the few women to rise above the level of beginner in aikido, she ran into problems that men do not meet and that tended to deepen her self-doubt and tear down the confidence she was struggling to build.

"The worst thing that ever happened was right after I'd been promoted to brown belt," Beth remembers. "I was beginning to think of myself as pretty strong and competent when a visiting instructor came to the school. He announced that he was going to teach a special advanced class, but when I asked him what time the class would meet, he said I couldn't come.

" 'Why not?' I asked.

" 'It's not for women,' he said.

" 'But I'm a brown belt.' I said. I just couldn't believe what I was hearing.

" 'It's not for women,' he repeated, looking at me as if I were crazy. 'And it's certainly not for mothers!'

"I began to fume and sputter out my objections. But he just glared at me.

" 'If you come to this class,' he said finally, 'you might get hurt.'

"There was no mistaking the tone in his voice. It was definitely threatening, and it worked. I didn't go to his class. I was afraid to. And I kept thinking that if I weren't such a coward, so afraid of getting hurt, I would've gone and really proven something, but that as it was, I was just a failure. It took me months to work my way out of the feeling of being a fool."

Nevertheless, Beth continued to train and to teach. Before long, she realized that she had become part of a historical movement that was coming into its own. "Women began coming to me to ask me to help them," she remembers. "Wherever I went, someone would ask me whether I could teach a workshop, give a course, do a demonstration. There were invitations to more events than I could keep track of."

By being just a little bit ahead of the wave, Beth became, to her own surprise, an important force in its development. "I knew a little bit at a time when women were beginning to realize that they knew nothing at all about self-defense and at a time when it was becoming an urgent priority for great numbers of women."

Two years after she inaugurated the self-defense course at the Venice Women's Center, Beth was awarded her black belt. Kris, eleven years old, was present at the ceremony. "We really are the best of friends," Beth says with a smile.

Soon afterwards, Beth and the other advanced students in the aikido club—all of whom were teaching classes of one kind or another—formed the Santa Monica Aikido Institute. Their instructor at the club agreed to be head instructor. He would teach them, and they would conduct classes for beginning and intermediate students.

In addition to the regular teachers, each of whom would teach

The sayu undo *(side to side) momentum throw, used against an attack in which both wrists have been grabbed from the front. When student Fritt Henley grabbed Beth's wrists, Beth stepped slightly toward and to the side of Fritt, moving her arms in a verticle circle as she did so. The lower arc of the circle drew Fritt forward and down; the upper arc tilted her backward, making it easy for Beth to force her to the ground.*

two or three classes a week, the institute needed a full-time person, a "resident" instructor, someone who would not only teach independently, but also assist the other teachers and handle the administration of the school. Beth wanted to do it—but there wouldn't be enough money to pay her a full salary. How would she and Kris live? When her older brother, with whom Kris had visited before, invited him to come east and attend school with his children for a term, everything fell into place. Kris was happy to go east and Beth, to save on rent, moved into the institute.

"To some people it might sound like a hardship," Beth says, smiling. "I kept my clothes in the women's dressing room and prepared my meals in the office. But to me it was heaven on earth. I woke up in the morning and did aikido, had breakfast and did aikido. In the afternoon, I taught aikido. In the evening, I trained. I couldn't have been happier."

Beth and the other instructors wanted the institute to be as open to the needs of their students as possible. They interviewed each person who enrolled to see what they wanted from their training. One of the women Beth interviewed had some very strong ideas.

"She was really impressed with me," Beth remembers. "I think I was the first woman black belt she'd ever met and she felt I should live up to what she called my 'station.' I thought I was doing pretty well just by being a black belt and an instructor. But she thought I had a lot more to offer and that I should teach a separate women's class."

Beth didn't think much of the idea at first. She had taught a self-defense class to women only. But she wasn't sure what the point of an all-women's aikido class would be. She agreed to ask the other women students how they felt about it. The response was overwhelmingly in favor.

"I still didn't really get it," Beth says. "I didn't know what they wanted. So at the first meeting, I asked them."

What they wanted, Beth learned, in addition to regular training, was a chance to deal with the problems they were having as women beginning a martial art. Some of them realized they were afraid of becoming strong, because that seemed so "unwomanly." Some were afraid of learning how to fight because that seemed so "masculine." They all needed help in learning how to trust themselves, how to be comfortable with their bodies, and how to deal with the self-doubts which threatened to stop them before they could even get started.

"One woman had begun a martial art once before, but she hadn't stayed with it," Beth remembers. "She had had an injury and been told by her instructor that women were really too delicate for martial arts training. Now we know that's just ridiculous, but if you throw that at a woman who's just beginning, it can be really

*B*eth *demonstrates a hold used to control an attacker after she has been thrown to the ground.*

devastating, and it had been for her. We spent a lot of time talking about the image of women as nature's weaklings and how much that image had hurt us. We all learned a lot in that class."

Above all, the women's class made Beth realize how important it was for women in the martial arts to know about one another. They needed one another, she felt, as models and sources of inspiration. As much for her own sake as for anyone else's, she decided to try to find other women martial artists who might be in the area.

Using phone books and newspapers, and following every lead that came her way, she compiled a list of all the martial arts schools she could find. Then she sent out letters—over two hundred of them. She said she was compiling a directory of black belt women and she asked all women who were interested to contact her.

Over thirty women responded, and Beth interviewed each one. She visited them in their schools, watched them train, spoke to them and to their instructors. A few of her own women students usually went with her. "It was so exciting and inspiring for us to find one another. Everyone was in favor of forming a permanent group of some kind. So I set up a meeting."

Women from just about every martial art attended. Instead of being divided by the differences in their arts, they felt drawn together as women martial artists. They decided to meet regularly, set up a newsletter, and work on projects that would strengthen them and help them reach out to other women. They called their group "Women in Martial Arts." Beth was asked to be president.

One of the first things WIMA organized was an all-day event featuring, in the morning, demonstrations of the various arts, and in the afternoon, workshops. Women could see all the arts and then take a workshop in the one that appealed to them the most. Over three hundred women attended the event. WIMA was off to a flying start.

About a year after WIMA was founded, Beth realized she would have to do something about her own training. She could not stay with her teacher. "It wasn't that he didn't have any more to teach me," she says now. "It was that he didn't think I should learn any more. As far as he was concerned, I knew as much as a woman needed to know. Today when a man tells me 'women don't do that,' or 'women don't need that,' I ask them how much experience they've had being a woman! I tell them I've had forty years experience, so I think I should be considered the expert! But at that time, I just decided to look elsewhere for training."

Beth applied to the institute in Japan that was the headquarters for her style of aikido. When she asked her teacher, as a courtesy, to write a letter of introduction for her, he refused.

"He made it very clear that he thought I was out of line," Beth says. "He said advanced training was not appropriate for women. I wasn't surprised, and I went ahead with my plans anyway. I arranged to work as a teacher of English to cover my expenses while I was there, and I gave Kris the choice of coming to Japan with me or going back to stay with my brother's family in Philadelphia. He chose to stay in the United States, and off I went."

Beth was happy to be able to study in the country in which aikido had been created. She immersed herself in the culture and she

trained almost every evening. But she felt alienated from the beginning.

"The women there were not taught to make their techniques
strong," she says. "Their techniques were supposed to be beautiful. They were told to 'dance' through the movement. I was much
more interested in aikido as self-defense. I cared about grace only if
it added to my technique, so I was going against the grain right
from the beginning, and there was quite a bit of disapproval."

On one occasion, Beth's partner was supposed to grab her and
she in turn was supposed to try to throw him down. But instead of
really grabbing her *gi*, he just touched her lightly.

"If someone isn't using any energy against you, it's very difficult
to do the technique," Beth explains. "So I said, 'More! Grab
more!' "

"My partner looked at me and grabbed just a little bit harder.

" 'No! No! Not enough!' I said. 'Grab harder!'

"I saw the moment at which he gave himself to the attack," she
says, "as if he were thinking, 'All right, if that's what she wants,
that's what she'll get!' Now, if you can move at just the moment a
person gives you their energy, you've got them, and I had him! I
just zapped right down, knocked the legs out from under him, and
he fell flat on his back with the most amazed look on his face! I got
up, and I bowed. I said, 'Thank you,' and went back to practicing
with other people. It was really fun!"

Eventually Beth gained the respect of the *sensei*, and the other
students treated her more seriously. Nevertheless, as a woman she
had to ask for things that were offered freely to men.

"Men were often invited to special sessions and special classes,"
she says. "And they were invited to stay after class to work on
special exercises. Sometimes I took it upon myself to ask whether it
might be possible for me to attend, too. When I did, I was usually
allowed to do so. But having to ask, having to put myself forward

The tenchi nage *(heaven and earth) throw, used here when Beth's wrists were grabbed from behind. Beth held one arm still, brought the other arm up, and turned toward her stationary arm so that she was beside her attacker (Sarah Falsey). As she turned, she brought the raised arm over Sarah's head, forcing her to the ground.*

in that way was very hard, and made me feel a lot of pressure to perform well. That's not the best way to learn or practice any-thing.''

On another occasion, Beth was watching two male students work on a technique she knew how to do quite well. The smaller man was unable to throw the larger man and Beth, usually smaller than her partner, saw just what the problem was.

"I knew that women were not supposed to interfere with what men were doing, but I finally took the bit between my teeth and decided that I wasn't going to just sit there. I walked over and said, 'Excuse me, but I think I can help you.'

"The smaller man had been trying to do a throw called *tenchi nage*—literally, the 'heaven-and-earth' throw. It is a momentum throw best used against someone who has grabbed you by both wrists. You step in and hold one hand down 'toward earth' and the other up 'toward heaven.' In that way you are spreading them apart and beginning to break their balance. You move in, raising your upper hand over and behind your opponent's head, and then you pull down, breaking their balance backwards so they land on their back. Your lower hand anchors them and keeps them grounded so they can't move out from the technique.

"I could see the point at which the smaller man was moving *in* rather than *up*, and I wanted to demonstrate what he was doing wrong. So I told the larger man to grab me, and I did the move the wrong way. The larger man stopped me from completing the technique. Then I wanted to do it the right way, so I told him to grab me again. I could see him setting himself in opposition to me. I could see in the stance he took that he was thinking, 'There's no way she's going to throw me!'

"But I was really clear about what I was doing. My ego wasn't on the line—I was teaching again. So I just said, 'This is the way you should do it—you go up, not in.' And I did it and it worked perfectly! Afterwards, they both thanked me."

Beth was promoted to second-degree black belt before she left Japan, a tribute to her accomplishments and an acknowledgment of her skill. Nevertheless, she was glad to be leaving.

"I had stuck it out," she says. "I had remained true to myself and my ideas. But I was very isolated and it was hard."

Back in the United States, Beth picked up Kris and the two took a leisurely six weeks to cross the country and return to California. She felt stronger, both physically and psychologically, than she had ever felt before because, as she says, "I had been through the fire."

In Santa Monica, Beth was soon teaching again, working part-time as a data processor, and using her organizational skills to form her own company, which presents self-defense workshops and products for women. Kris and Beth were the models for the self-defense photograph that was sent everywhere. "It became our favorite family picture," she says now.

Beth and her son, Chris, demonstrate a self-defense strategy.

Beth still lives in California. She says she will continue training and teaching for the rest of her life. The work has gone out of it now, and it has become a pure joy. "I really started out behind the eight ball. But my body has become like a finely tuned instrument. It demands to be used, and when it is used, it is a sheer physical joy. I am addicted to the martial arts now, and I like to imagine that I will be just as sprightly when I am eighty years old. I tell my students what I have learned myself, that martial arts training is training in personal growth. You learn that you can cope with things, that you have strengths and inner resources to call upon, and that you don't have to do things out of fear. You are always stretching yourself, testing your limits, pushing them back. You really are confronting yourself on the mat, and what you learn there changes your entire life."

The
Universal Way

THE TWENTIETH CENTURY HAS BEEN A TIME OF UNPRECEDENTED EXPANSION for all the martial arts. They have been carried from Asia to every continent on earth, to people of almost every culture. Although most martial artists around the world prefer to work within long-established styles and systems, some have chosen to work on their own. This is part of the martial tradition. There has always been room for new forms and for people who choose to create them.

Bruce Lee, one of the greatest and certainly the most popular martial artist of our time, began his career by practicing *wing-chun* kung fu, an art created by a sixteenth-century Buddhist nun. After feeling his own authority as a martial artist, he went on to create his own style, *jeet kune do*, the Way of the Intercepting Fist. Although Lee was an anti-traditionalist in many ways, in this he was part of a tradition.

The martial arts offer an experience, not a final achievement. They are processes, not products; martial artists never stop learning. That is why a person can train with devotion and discipline for a lifetime. It is why some people can work on movements

160

and forms that have been prescribed for centuries and never feel that they are stale. It is why others, starting from established styles and systems, go on to improvise, experiment, and design styles of their own. Tonie Harris is one such artist. The Universal Way is her style.

TONIE HARRIS

onie Harris began her study of the martial arts in 1972, after seeing Bruce Lee fight in *Enter the Dragon.*

"I had to learn how to do that," Tonie says, "or die trying. If I could have, I would have become Bruce Lee."

Tonie was twenty-five at the time and married, the mother of two-year-old twins, with hardly any time to call her own and no money at all. "But I was determined," she says. "I had seen something I really wanted, and I couldn't get it out of my mind."

After months of looking, Tonie found a school called Karate for Women, established by the Oregon Karate Association and run by Paula and Pauline Short (two-thirds of a set of triplets). The Shorts wanted to make the martial arts available to as many women as possible, so the fees at Karate for Women were very low. Tonie paid twelve dollars a month for as many classes as she could get to—and she got to at least three a week. In the beginning, she always arrived late, because she wanted to miss the exercises with which the classes began. She wanted to fly through the air like Bruce Lee, fell opponents with ease, and come out on top against overwhelming odds. She didn't want to do leg raises and push-ups.

"I didn't have any physical problems," she says now. "I had a listening problem. I thought I knew what they were going to tell me, so I didn't pay any attention. All I wanted to hear about was when I was going to get my black belt!"

Today Tonie can deliver flying crescent kicks worthy of Lee himself. She can fell opponents with ease. And she has come out on top in spite of what can only be called overwhelming odds. She is a superb martial artist, a teacher, trainer, and champion with fifty-eight trophies to her credit after six years of tournament competition. She is also a devout born-again Christian, whose strength and warmth touch everyone who meets her, and the mother of four lively children whom she is raising on her own. She also works full-time for the Portland, Oregon, Public Schools System.

"Sounds tiring, doesn't it?" she says with a chuckle. "It is! But God gives me the strength, praise the Lord."

Tonie was born in Portland Oregon on the first day of summer, June 21, 1947. "I love my birthday," she says. "I love having been born at a time when there is such a strong feeling of life and creation everywhere."

Her infancy was not an easy one. Her mother, barely seventeen when Tonie was born, was already separated from her equally young husband. Overwhelmed and deeply distressed, she placed her newborn daughter in an orphanage and left Oregon for Alaska. When Tonie was eighteen months old, her grandparents gained custody of her and were able to bring her home with them. Her aunt Marion, fourteen years old at the time, took care of her while her grandparents were at work. The household was an unusual one, but it was filled with love. Tonie, healthy and bright, blossomed.

"I was a daredevil as a kid. There was nothing I wouldn't try and I wasn't afraid of anyone. By the time I was four, my grandfather had nicknamed me 'Brat.' And I was a brat. How could I help it! I never had to share anything or learn about taking turns, or learn how to be second—or third, or fourth, the way my kids do."

During Special Training 1983, held in Lawrenceville, New Jersey, Tonie works on a form she is developing for her style.

There was never any extra money, so everyone learned to make do, and make over, and most of all, not to care too much about the things that money can buy.

"Sure, I like material comfort," Tonie says now. "Who doesn't? But I know that's not what really counts. It's okay with me if my neighbors have more than I do. It's okay if they have a pool— they're not going to take that pool to heaven. And besides, there's a river down the road somewhere!"

As a teenager, Tonie thought of herself as "average." She liked most of her high school classes, worked hard when she wanted to, loved sports, wasted lots of time, and got along well with just about everybody. One of a handful of blacks in a high school of twenty-five hundred, Tonie doesn't remember having any special problems.

"I was taught not to take things personally," she says. "And that probably saved me from a lot of confusion. My grandmother used to say that I should always 'consider the source' and not let other people get me down. In any case, I didn't have too much trouble figuring out who I was. But I had a terrible time figuring out where I was going."

College was not an option for Tonie. Without any clear idea of what she wanted to do, or could do, she floated from one job to another after high school.

"Nothing seemed right," she says. "I had to work because I had to earn money, but I couldn't find a job or a place that made sense to me."

At one point she enrolled in a career training school with the vague idea of learning about skin care and cosmetics. She dropped out without finishing the program. Too bright and energetic to settle, not knowing where to turn for guidance, Tonie drifted. When she was twenty, she married. "I guess I hoped that being married would be the answer, but of course it wasn't. Instead, I felt as though I had jumped from the frying pan into the fire."

Tonie's husband, Franklin Harris, was a hard-working man, but he had what Tonie calls "old-fashioned" ideas. Eleven years older than his wife, he didn't understand her restlessness, and he didn't want to hear about it.

"When I say 'old-fashioned,' " Tonie explains, "I don't mean 'good old-fashioned!' My husband thought women were second to men in every way. He thought I wouldn't have any problems if I would just concentrate on making him happy, the way a wife was supposed to do."

Tonie found herself more adrift than ever. In the fall of 1968, she met Michaela Sutphin, who introduced her to Christianity in a "brand-new way." She and her husband grew even farther apart.

"I was raised a Christian," Tonie says, "but it wasn't until I met Michaela that it became important to me. I believe now that God was dealing with me through her. He was trying to help me get my direction down. And I did. I felt like I was born again and I started growing, and that made things between Franklin and me much, much worse."

Tonie's husband resisted the change in her. He didn't share her feelings or her beliefs, and he didn't want her to be involved with something in which he had no part. They clashed again and again, more and more unhappily. Then twin sons were born to them, and things seemed to take a turn for the better.

"The boys, Jocala and Franklin, were just such a joy. They were something we could really share. It seemed we might be able to make a go of our marriage after all. We saw *Enter the Dragon* together—and afterwards, when I said I wanted to take a martial art, Franklin said he thought I should go ahead and look for a school!"

Tonie quickly became serious about her training. "I had always been athletic," she says, "and I liked every sport I ever learned how to play. But this was different. I was learning how to fight—it wasn't a game. It felt really good to know I could defend myself. And it was all easy for me. I never felt awkward. But my gift, if I had a gift, was that I wanted to do it so much. I went all the time. As much as I could be there, I was there."

"I was real cocky, too," Tonie says. "After two months, I thought I could take on anybody and I got right out there with this brown belt. I took a back kick to my stomach that I can still feel. What a shock! But it was just what I needed, because after that I understood why you have to be disciplined, and that you have to work to get those skills. It was just about then that my husband Franklin thought I had learned enough! I wouldn't have stopped for anything."

Tonie was pregnant when she began to train, although she didn't know it at the time. She earned her green belt just before Tonie Lamont, her third son, was born. She took a few months off then, and she took a few months off three years later when her daughter Diane was born. "Except for that, I don't think I ever missed two weeks in a row," she says now.

She hardly ever missed a demonstration or a tournament either, and had begun to win competitions even before she received her black belt in April, 1977. Although the belt had been her goal when she started, by the time she got it, she wanted more. She under-

Tonie explains sparring strategies as her students watch.

stood that the skill displayed by masters—including people like Bruce Lee—is the result not of physical techniques alone but of mental strengths and sensitivities that take years to develop. Black belt rank, as her teacher explained, means that you have a good foundation and are ready to begin advanced study. Tonie was ready. She felt stronger and more confident than ever. She was ready to come to terms with her marriage, too.

"We were at the point where it felt like do or die," she says, "and our struggle was poisoning everything. I was beginning to find myself for the first time in my life, and my husband just didn't want me to. I have to say I was afraid. I was definitely afraid. I could hardly imagine how I would make a home for the kids on my own. But sometimes you have to take that risk and go, and in the fall of

1977, a few months after I got my black belt, I picked up the kids and left."

With Franklin and Jocala eight years old, Tonie Lamont five, and Diane going on three, Tonie returned to her grandmother and the house where she herself had been raised.

"We stayed there for about six months, until I got myself together and could figure out what to do," she says. "That may sound like a negative time, but it wasn't at all. I was on my own at last, and I knew I would find my way."

Later that year, Tonie left Karate for Women. "I didn't know exactly what I was looking for," she says, "but I knew it was time to move on."

Over the next three years, Tonie studied almost every fighting art offered in the Portland, Oregon, area. She studied *kempo* karate, street-fighting, and Philippine stick-fighting with Ali Mohammed, whose strenuous and challenging classes are legendary in Portland.

She studied wrestling with Roy Pittman, Recreational Director and wrestling instructor at Peninsula Community Park and coach at Portland Community College. Tonie learned how to fall from Roy, and she learned how to avoid falling, how to lower her center of gravity so she would be able to stand up against almost any amount of force—like the children's toys that spring back up no matter how far over you tip them, because they have weighted bottoms.

"Roy taught me how to move, how to pivot, how to shift my weight and keep it low, no matter what, so that I couldn't be toppled," she says.

She studied American free style karate with Dan Anderson of the Anderson Karate Studio. From him she learned some of her most powerful kicks.

"I'm not naturally very limber," Tonie says. "In fact, that was my greatest weakness when I began. We'd do a split and I'd be three

While her students spar in place to music, which Tonie hopes will help them keep their movements fluid and relaxed, she practices some of her own favorite moves.

feet from the floor. I didn't think I would ever be able to do a decent side kick or hook kick, so I just concentrated on front and round kicks, and on hand techniques. But with Dan, I really improved my flexibility. He helped me develop a set of exercises for stretching, which I still do, and I got my side and hook kicks just the way I want them. I hardly ever use anything else now."

Sometimes, when Tonie was temporarily without a teacher and a place to train, she worked out alone in the basement of the building in which she lived, or in the park, or in the gym of the local public school.

"It got so the kids in the neighborhood wanted to spar with me whenever they saw me," she recalls. "If I had the time, I always would. We'd fight a little here and a little there. I'd give them pointers. Some of them got to be pretty good. Now when I walk through the streets the kids all call me *sensei*."

Her own children sometimes call her *sensei*, too. "They're all into the martial arts," she says. "They don't have much of a choice with a mom like me. Sometimes they don't want to do it, but I think the discipline is good for them."

   As Tonie studied with one teacher and then another, she incorporated the things she was learning until she was practicing a unique kind of art that was essentially her own. It had elements from each of the styles and arts she studied, but it wasn't identical with any of them. It was fast, graceful, and very effective. With it, Tonie piled up titles and trophies from local, regional, and national competitions.

   "I really like fighting," Tonie says. "Maybe that's what makes me a good fighter. I like using strategy. I like to make my opponent move, control the space and the shots. In the beginning, I depended mostly on force. I got my moves in because I was always willing to take chances and I wasn't afraid of getting hurt. Now I think I've really come into my own. I can fight without getting hurt and without hurting anyone else. It's fun!"

   Karate Illustrated named Tonie the Top Female *Karateka* in the

Tonie demonstrates free-sparring. She thinks she is a good fighter at least partly because she enjoys it so much.

Northwest in 1979. That same year, she began to work in a local elementary school as an office clerk. "I felt like Wonder Woman in disguise," she says.

The school had a lot of troubled children, and Tonie thought martial arts training would be good for them. She applied to the board of education and was granted a provisional certificate to work in physical education because of her "credibility" as a martial artist.

The program Tonie set up was more successful than she had hoped. Working with seven or eight children at a time, she taught them stances, postures, hand and leg techniques, forms. Three of them learned to break boards. All of them came early, wanted to stay late, and asked Tonie for additional exercises they could work on at home and on weekends.

"They were so responsive and they worked so hard," Tonie says. "The changes they went through were really something to see. And when I realized what was happening, I wanted everyone to see them! A few months into the school year, I got in touch with the board of education again because I had heard that they could arrange to send us someone who could get those kids on film."

The Portland board, through the Office of Talented and Gifted Children, sent Susan Susak, a filmmaker, to work with Tonie's class. The sixth-, seventh-, and eighth-graders worked "energetically, intelligently, and well" throughout the shooting. They helped with many behind-the-scenes decisions. The film that resulted bears witness to the hard work and progress of children who had been considered almost unteachable.

"People could hardly believe it when it was finished," Tonie says. "These were the kids they said couldn't concentrate and had no discipline. The film showed that they could and they did. It showed every level of hard work, stress, and struggle. They were terrific, and the film showed it!"

It has since been presented in several Oregon schools. Last year

Tonie leads an exercise in which eyes are closed and the emphasis is on developing an awareness of your body's position in space—the level of your punches and kicks, the distance you cover with each step forward and backward—without seeing it.

requests for copies were received from schools in Pennsylvania and Virginia.

Tonie is still teaching schoolchildren, and now she is teaching adults as well. In 1981, after three years of training with teachers from various arts and styles, she was invited to be a trainer herself at the Fifth Annual Special Training Camp for women in the martial arts. It was organized by Joan Nelson's Feminist Self-Defense and Karate Association of Lansing, Michigan. Tonie's workshop focused on free-sparring exercises and on sensory awareness drills.

"I had the women pair off," she explains. "One had to close her eyes, the other kept hers open. The one with her eyes open attacked in slow motion, and the other had to react. She had to really concentrate and monitor what was going on with her whole body—because she couldn't use her eyes. She had to feel what was coming at her, use that inner being inside her to sense and respond. Later, both partners were blindfolded and they had to spar. I'd guide them back toward one another if they got too far apart, but that didn't happen much. It was a good exercise, and I think it showed everyone that we have sensory powers we don't even know about because we never ask ourselves to use them."

Tonie's workshops generated lots of excitement among the participants. She was buoyed and elated on the flight home. "I was sitting next to the woman who had led a workshop in t'ai chi,"she recalls. "We were talking about the spiritual side of the martial arts, and the kind of energy that is involved. I was looking out the window as we talked, looking at the clouds, feeling very close to heaven, and I realized that what I really wanted was a martial art that was universal, an art that would be for all people. I just looked at the clouds and the blue sky, and I thought, I don't want labels or divisions. I want something that includes everything and is for everyone. She knew the Chinese words for what I was talking about, and to me they sounded beautiful: *Yu Chu Tao*, the Universal Way."

On her return to Portland, Tonie began to teach her art, the Universal Way, to women and men. Now she is making plans to form her own school. She has also begun to work with a new teacher, Master Somsack, a Laotian and the founder, in 1980, of the

Laos Martial Arts Association. Tonie loved the high, forceful kicks and the strong stances of Master Somsack's art the first time she saw them in a neighborhood demonstration.

"I was trying to do one of the kicks when I got home," she recalls, "and having plenty of trouble, too. Then I looked up the street—and there was Master Somsack himself coming toward me!"

As it turned out, Master Somsack had just moved into a house across the street from Tonie's. He had noticed the trophies in her window and been looking forward to meeting "the man" they belonged to, thinking that "he" must be very good.

"Well, 'he' was me," Tonie says, "and we had a good laugh about that."

Tonie has been studying with Master Somsack ever since. "I respect his art and his methods. He has a lot to teach me. He knows I'm working on my own style, and that I have my own students, and that's just fine with him. There's no end to what you can learn in the martial arts, and no end to what you have to give to others."

Tonie is working harder than ever now, teaching children, teaching adults, developing her own sets and forms, training with Master Somsack, raising her daughter and three sons.

"I feel like one of the most fortunate people on earth," she says, "and I want to pass it along. I want to give people the ability to defend themselves, I want to give them pride, and I want to teach them to overcome fear. I feel like I can, because I've done those things in my own life. I want to teach my students to go down the good road spiritually and physically through self-discipline, self-confidence, and self-respect—as well as respect for all other people. I don't know whether they'll have classes in the martial arts in heaven, but if they do, I hope the good Lord uses me."

Suggestions for
Further Reading

Boslooper, Thomas, and Hayes, Margaret. *The Femininity Game.* New York: Stein and Day, 1974.
A thoughtful analysis of the meaning of sports in our culture, the reasons and ways in which women have been kept out of them.

Corcoran, John, and Farkas, Emil. *The Complete Martial Arts Catalogue.* New York: Simon and Schuster, 1977.
Over 200 pages of information about the various arts, people in them, events, milestones. Photographs too, and an easy-to-read question and answer format. This book is fun.

Delacoste, Frederique, and Newman, Felice. *Fight Back!* Minneapolis: Cleis Press, 1981.
A compendium of essays, fiction, documents, personal testimony, and strategies concerning ways in which women have resisted and can resist violence and abuse.

Draeger, Don, and Smith, Robert W. *Comprehensive Asian Fighting Arts.* New York: Kodasha International, 1981.
The definitive sourcebook, this is a scholarly and authoritative encyclopedia of the martial arts. The history of the arts, their development, their masters are presented in rich detail. Illustrated with rare and unusual photographs and plates.

Kaplan, Janice, *Women and Sports.* New York: Avon, 1979.
The most informative, provocative, and encouraging book around covering almost every aspect of the athletic experience vis-a-vis women. Also facts about nutrition, women's physiology and capabilities. This book will be a classic in the field.

Kauz, Herman. *The Martial Spirit.* Woodstock, New York: Overlook Press, 1977.
An introduction to the martial arts from the point of view of the practitioner: what the arts feel like, what each has to offer the student. Interesting discussions, good photographs.

Minick, Michael. *The Wisdom of Kung Fu.* New York: William Morrow and Company, 1974.
The history, development, values, and ideas behind the Chinese martial arts, including a unique collection of "sayings of the masters."

Payne, Peter. *Martial Arts: The Spiritual Dimension.* New York: The Crossroad Publishing Company, 1981.
Fascinating and informative exploration of the martial arts as spiritual, psychological, and "psychophysical" disciplines. Extraordinary photographs.

Ribner, Susan, and Chin, Richard. *The Martial Arts.* New York: Harper and Row, 1978.
The best introduction to the martial arts, their origin, development, essential features, modern versions. Anecdotes, descriptions of training, drawings, and prints, too.

PERIODICALS

Fighting Woman News. Valerie Eads, Editor. Box 1459 Grand Central Station, New York, N.Y. 10163
All the news there is about women in the martial arts, in combat sports, and in self-defense, including coverage of events, information about schools, historical essays, book reviews, product reviews, how-to's, photographs, prints, and a miscellany of other interesting items.

Resources

National Woman's Martial Arts Federation
POB 229
East Lansing, Michigan
44823

Women in martial arts
12538 Venice Boulevard
Mar Vista, California
90066

Index

Aikido, 13, 125, 126, 140–141, 143–159
Amateur Athletic Union (AAU), 31, 32, 41, 43, 130
American Sports for Israel Committee, 44, 45
Anderson, Dan, 169–170
Anderson Karate Studio, 169
Athens (Ohio) Mental Health Center, 97
Austin, Beth, 143–159

Banshee, 19
Bates, Gilbert, 78, 79, 81
Bates, LaVerne, 67, 69–81
Bates Kung Fu Studio, 79–80
Black Belt Magazine, 80, 129, 131
Black Belt Woman, 131, 132
Bodhidharma, 2
Bokken, 120
Boxing, white crane, 3
Braziel, Maureen, 41, 43
British Women's Judo Open, 43–44
Brooklyn Women's Martial Arts, 49, 62–63

Chang San-feng, 83
Ch'i, 65, 82, 83

Chiang, Meeyalin, 80
Choi, Joon P., 107
Choi, Young P., 107, 108
Coney Island Apaches, 29

Dacanay, Pattie, 85–99
Dunckle, Margaret, 7

Eads, Valerie, 121, 123–139
Eastern United States Kendo Federation, 138, 139
Ederle, Gertrude, 6
Ellman, Annie, 14, 47, 49–64
Empty-handed fighting. *See* Tae kwan do
Evoy, Al, 30, 31

Fa Mulan ("Magnolia"), 3
Feminists in Self-Defense Training (FIST), 114
Fifer, Gerry, 12–13
Fighting Woman News, 131, 138, 139
Funakoshi, Gichin, 47

Goman, Toni, 107, 110
Graff, Sunny, 101, 103–118

178

Harper, Phyllis, 35–36
Harris, Dorothy, 6
Harris, Tonie, 161, 163–175
Heran Games, 131–132
Ho, Nathaniel, 80
Hwarang-do, 101

International Kendo Federation, 134
Interpretation of strength, 83
Ishizuka, Kanichi, 126, 132–133
Ishizuka, Mozart, 136
Itagaki, 4

Javorek, Dr. Frank, 15
Jeet kune do, 160
"*Jiptjung,*" 100
Judo, 4, 5, 6, 8, 12, 18, 23–25, 27–45
Jujutsu, 24, 101

Kaizuka, Kunimitsu, 136
Kano, Jigaro, 4, 24, 38
Kano, Risei, 38
Kanokogi, Rusty, 8, 25, 27–45
Kanokogi, Ryohei, 40–41
Kaplan, Janice, 8
Karate, 5, 8–9, 10, 12, 13, 14, 18, 46–47,
    49–64, 100, 169
Karate for Women, 163, 169
Kata, 39, 46, 60, 64
Katame-no-kata, 39
Keiko, 127, 128
Kelly, Roberta Trias, 20
Kendo, 17, 119–121, 123–139
Kenjutsu, 119, 120
Ki, 46, 65
Kiai, 46–47
Kingston, Maxine Hong, 2
Kodokan, the, 4, 24, 36–38

Krasner, Lee, 27–28
Kung fu, 3, 64, 65–67, 69–81
    ship pal gi, 108
    wing-chun, 3, 160
    See also T'ai chi ch'uan
Kyushu Judo School (Brooklyn), 40

Lao Tsu, 2, 83, 99
Laos Martial Arts Association, 175
Lee, Bruce, 4, 6, 160, 163, 164, 168
Leong, John S. S., 87–90, 98

Maccabiah Games, 44
Makikomi, 33
Martial arts, historic background of,
    1–8
Matilda, Countess, 123, 139
McLaughlin, Bob, 130
Mohammed, Ali, 169
Motor Maids of America, 124
Musashi, Miyamoto, 120

Nage-no-kata, 39
Naginata, 4, 129
National Center for the Prevention
    and Control of Rape, 111
National Women's Martial Arts
    Federation, 19–20
Nelson, Joan, 174
New York Buddhist Academy Kendo
    Club, 123, 126
New York Karate School for Women,
    21
Niggle, Barbara, 21

Olympics, 6, 25, 44, 45, 131–132
Orange, Gerald, 58, 59, 60, 62
Oregon Karate Association, 163

Oriental Martial Arts College, 107,
    108, 110–111, 114, 118
Oyama, Mas, 5–6

Pan American Tae Kwon Do Games,
    117
Pennsylvania Ballet, 124
Pittman, Roy, 169
Push-hands, 93, 95
Push-ups, 10, 21

Randori, 32, 37, 38
Ribner, Susan, 10, 11, 12, 14, 21
Roosevelt, Theodore, 24

Saiganji, Mamaru, 33, 35, 36
Santa Monica Aikido Institute,
    150–152
Schine, Roberta, 21
Selkin, Dr. James, 15
Shaolin Temple, 2
Shigekawa, Joan, 129, 130
Shinai, 119, 120, 127, 128, 133, 137
Ship pal gi, 108
Short, Paula, 163
Short, Pauline, 163
Shotokan, the, 47
Sil lum p'ai, 75
Somsack, Master, 174–175
Songdok, Queen, 100
Strange, Pat, 35
Susak, Susan, 172
Sutphin, Michaela, 166
Switzer, Kathrine, 7–8, 11
Swordfighting, 119–121, 123–139. *See
    also* Kendo

Tae kwon do, 5, 18, 100–101, 103–118

T'ai chi ch'uan, 65, 67, 82–83, 85–99
Taoism, 66, 83, 98
Telsey, Nadia, 8–9, 12, 13, 58, 60, 62,
    64
Temple for Physical and Spiritual
    Survival, 58
Third World Kendo Championships,
    134
Tomoé, 4
Trias, Robert, 5, 20
Tsheng, Sifu, 92–95

United States Karate Association, 5
Universal Way, 160–161, 163–175
Uyeshiba, Morihei, 141

Venice, California, Women's Center,
    147

Way of the Intercepting Fist, 160
White crane boxing, 3
Wing-chun kung fu, 3, 160
Women Against Rape (WAR), 106,
    107, 111, 112, 113
Women in Martial Arts (WIMA), 154
Women's Action Collective, 106, 114
Women's Martial Arts Union, 12, 15,
    17, 18, 19, 58
Wong, Ark Yuey, 78, 80
Woo, Fenia, 74–76, 78, 80
World Tae Kwon Do Federation, 101,
    103
World T'ai Chi Association, 95

Young Lords, 54
Yu Chu Tao. See Universal Way

Zaharias, Babe Didrikson, 6

Acknowledgments

THIS BOOK WAS A LONG TIME IN THE MAKING, AND MANY PEOPLE HELPED A GREAT deal along the way. I would like to thank, first of all, the women whose stories are presented here. This book is meant to celebrate their achievements. It is also meant to honor the many other women martial artists at work today. Their stories could fill another book, another dozen books. If I could, I would write about them all.

For their help, suggestions, and kind consideration, I would like to thank Susan Murcott of the *Kahawai Journal of Women and Zen,* and Michael Minick, author and student of the Chinese martial arts. My special thanks to Professor C. N. Tay of the Hagop Kevorkian Center of Near Eastern Studies of New York University for sharing his time and knowledge of Chinese history and culture with me.

It is my pleasure to thank my editor, Donna Brooks, for her faith in this project; Nancy Rosenblum, California photographer, for coming to the rescue in the nick of time; Morgen Gwenwald, New York photographer, for her kindness and heartening spirit of sisterhood; Randy Meadoff, for her good counsel; Gerry Fifer, for sharing her story and her photigraphs; my friend Gudrun Fonfa, for her good advice and her good heart; and my friend Barbara Cortes, for her company and for some of the best conversations I've ever had. My lasting thanks to Susan Ribner, author and martial artist, who shared her thoughts and her files with me, made it easy for me to call, and always found time to help.

Finally, I want to thank my son, Willie, for his understanding and enthusiasm; my daughter, Sara, for her sunny ways; and the women with whom I train in karate for being the inspiration of a lifetime.

50   25